A Wealthier, Fairer Scotland

The Political Economy of Constitutional Change

edited by Michael Keating

EDINBURGH
University Press

Edinburgh University Press is one of the leading university presses in the UK. We publish academic books and journals in our selected subject areas across the humanities and social sciences, combining cutting-edge scholarship with high editorial and production values to produce academic works of lasting importance. For more information visit our website: edinburghuniversitypress.com

Edinburgh University Press Ltd
The Tun – Holyrood Road
12(2f) Jackson's Entry
Edinburgh EH8 8PJ

Typeset in 11/13 Sabon by
Servis Filmsetting Ltd, Stockport, Cheshire,
printed and bound in Great Britain by
CPI Group (UK) Ltd, Croydon CR0 4YY

A CIP record for this book is available from the British Library

ISBN 978 1 4744 1642 9 (hardback)
ISBN 978-1-4744-1643-6 (paperback)
ISBN 978-1-4744-1644-3 (webready PDF)
ISBN 978-1-4744-1645-0 (epub)

Contents

Figures

Tables

Contributors

Michael Keating is Professor of Politics at the Universities of Aberdeen and Edinburgh.

David Bell is Professor of Economics at the University of Stirling.

Paul Cairney is Professor of Politics at the University of Stirling.

David Eiser is Research Fellow in Economics at the University of Stirling.

Malcolm Harvey is Teaching Fellow in Politics at the University of Aberdeen.

Patrizio Lecca is Research Fellow in Economics at the University of Strathclyde.

Robert Liñeira is Research Fellow in Politics at the University of Edinburgh.

Katerina Lisenkova is Senior Research Fellow at the National Institute of Economic and Social Research.

Craig McAngus is Lecturer in Politics at the University of Aberdeen.

Nicola McEwen is Professor of Politics at the University of Edinburgh.

Peter G. McGregor is Emeritus Professor of Economics at University of Strathclyde.

Kirstein Rummery is Professor of Social Policy at the University of Stirling.

Emily St Denny is Research Assistant in Politics at the University of Stirling.

Kim Swales is Emeritus Professor of Economics at University of Strathclyde.

Preface

In 2014, Scotland voted against independence but, following a pledge by the unionist parties, it then received additional powers over taxation and welfare. Added to existing powers devolved in 1999 and 2012, the Scotland Act (2016) endowed Scotland with the competences, potentially, to fulfil its ambition to create a wealthier and fairer nation. This book examines how this might be possible in practice. It will be of interest not only to students of Scotland but to all concerned with the potential of small nations and regions to master their own fates in a complex, multilevel world.

The book is the product of an interdisciplinary project in the Centre on Constitutional Change, funded by an Economic and Social Research Council grant, ES/L003325/1. The first book from this project (Keating 2017) examined the issues in the referendum debate, including institutions, economics, welfare and taxation and spending. This book looks to the future, returning to some of the same issues and asking how they might be resolved. Scotland's future constitutional status remains, at the time of writing, unresolved. The implications of UK withdrawal from the EU are unclear. As the chapters in this book show, the 2016 settlement, the result of a political compromise rather than a measured analysis of policy requirements, may not provide an optimal outcome. Whatever the political future, however, the question of how to reconcile economic growth with social justice and cohesion will remain.

Michael Keating
Aberdeen and Edinburgh
July 2016

1 The Political Economy of Devolution

Michael Keating

Scotland after the referendum

The Scottish independence referendum of 2014 was a momentous event, which engaged the political class and the general public like few political events before it. The question on the ballot paper was, in appearance, a simple one with a straightforward answer, whether Scotland should be an independent country. A second question, on more devolution or a radical rearrangement of Scotland's relationship with the UK, was explicitly ruled out. Yet in practice, the two sides showed a degree of convergence on precisely this middle ground. One reason was that, as our research showed, public opinion was strongly clustered there (Liñeira, Henderson and Delaney 2017). Another was that, in the modern world, nations are interdependent and old ideas about sovereignty hide the limitations in the freedom of action of all but the most powerful states. So the debate moved quickly from dry constitutional issues to economic and social policy and how Scotland could achieve better outcomes, either in or out of the Union; it is this that accounts for the reach of the debate into civil society. Another feature of the Scottish debate was that it mostly did not pit different visions of future society against each other but rehearsed ways of achieving much the same goals. The two main parties in Scotland, while divided on constitutional matters, shared the same broadly social democratic ideology, while the Conservatives stayed in the political centre. Only a minority of voices called for a market-liberal model of state in which taxes would be cut and the scope of the public sector radically curtailed. So what the debate hinged on was whether large or small states are economically more efficient or whether social justice was better conceptualised and achieved at a UK or a Scottish scale. These issues are covered in another of our books, *Debating Scotland* (Keating 2017).

The referendum was followed by the Smith Commission. This was an all-party body set up to meet a pledge (the 'vow') made by the unionist parties in the last stage of the campaign to give Scotland more devolved powers but building on earlier work by the parties themselves. The resulting legislation (the Scotland Act, 2016) provides for more control over taxation and welfare, although stopping short of full devolution of these fields. Added to existing powers over economic development, infrastructure, education, training and research, these give Scotland a range of instruments to shape both its economic future and its welfare settlement. The question addressed in this book is what it can do with these powers. This was an important strand in our interdisciplinary research project on the constitutional future of Scotland. We did not see independence and union as stark alternatives but rather as a spectrum, with different combinations of powers at each point in the range. The new division of powers may not be optimal and it was more the result of political compromise than deep analysis. There are likely to be further changes in the future, but it is useful at this point to move the debate on from what powers there should be to how they should be used.

The story of devolution in Scotland has been one of a progression from limited administrative decentralisation in the form of the Scottish Office, founded in 1885 to give more coherence to Scottish administration. Over the subsequent century, the Scottish Office extended its reach to cover most domestic policy with the big exceptions of taxation and social security but remained a department of central government, following the broad policy lines set down in London (Midwinter, Keating and Mitchell 1991). The proposals for a legislative assembly in the failed Scotland Act of 1978 would have granted Scotland more autonomy on public service provision but reserved taxation, economic policy, social security and redistributive policies generally. The Scotland Act (1998), which set up the present Scottish Parliament, was more generous. It specifies not the devolved powers (as in the 1978 Act) but those reserved to the centre, leaving everything else to Scotland (although subject to European laws in some fields). Unlike the 1978 Act, it devolved important instruments for economic development such as regional development grants and Scottish Enterprise, but retained nearly all tax and welfare powers. The only tax power granted to the Scottish Parliament, the ability to change the standard rate of income tax by three pence in the pound, was never used.

The Scotland Act of 2012, which resulted from the report of the Calman Commission following the narrow victory of the Scottish National Party (SNP) at the Scottish elections of 2011, conceded greater control over taxes but was overtaken by the 2016 Act. The Scottish Parliament will now set the rates and bands for the whole of income tax on earned income, although not on dividends or capital gains. Half the value added tax (VAT) from Scotland will be assigned to it, meaning that it will receive the money but not set the rates (EU law has hitherto not permitted this). The 2016 Act also brought the Scottish Parliament into the sphere of welfare. It will take control of a series of welfare benefits and have the power to create new benefits within devolved fields and to top up benefits reserved to the UK. The unionist parties have claimed that this will give Scotland one of the most powerful devolved governments in the world. It is very difficult to test this claim, as devolution is a multidimensional concept, but there has certainly been a substantial transfer of power.

The powers of the Scottish Parliament and Government are now nearer to the scale of their ambition, as set out in the Scottish Government's National Performance Framework, introduced by the SNP when it came to power in 2007. The strategic aim is a Scotland that is 'Wealthier, Fairer, Healthier, Safer and Stronger, Smarter and Greener'. In a sense these objectives might look rather banal as it is difficult to imagine anyone supporting their opposite and they are not so different from the objectives of the preceding Labour/Liberal Democrat administration. What is significant is that these objectives take us beyond the 'regional devolution' model of government to match the ambitions of nation states themselves. Yet Scotland is not alone here, and its experience provides insight to larger issues of relevance to other states in Europe and beyond. Key policy fields including economic development and welfare are being transformed in response to social and demographic change and rescaled, shifting from the nation state to the global and European level and at the same time downwards to the local and intermediate level.

The Keynesian Welfare State

The post-war era saw a distinct political economy emerge in the states of western Europe, sometimes characterised as the Keynesian Welfare State. Keynesian demand management seemed to resolve the macroeconomic problem, securing steady growth and full employment. National economic planning could ensure provision of infrastructure and accommodate a growing population. National economic policy was matched by a growing welfare state organised within the same boundaries. Growth and welfare were seen as complementary since expansion of education, health and other public services enhanced the quality of the workforce at a time when skills were becoming important. The Keynesian Welfare State represented a social compromise between capital and labour on mutually beneficial terms, predicated on the existence of national borders, which locked in capital and labour, which were not easily able to relocate outside the state altogether. National welfare states also rested upon a shared identity or social citizenship, which created an affective solidarity (Marshall 1992).

There was a territorial dimension to all this. In what has been called 'spatial Keynesianism', regional policies were used to divert investment to underdeveloped and declining regions, through grants, tax incentives, infrastructure provision and development controls. Equalisation grants ensured that poorer regions could provide public services at the same level as wealthy ones and, in a way that is difficult to understand now, central governments pressed local governments to spend more, rather than less. This could all be presented as a positive-sum game. Poor regions gained from investment, wealthy regions saw congestion reduced, and the national economy mobilised otherwise idle resources.

During the Keynesian welfare era, there was a widespread assumption in favour of centralisation. Large centralised states could manage macroeconomic stability, redistribute resources socially and geographically and provide a safeguard against asymmetrical shocks, that is economic downturns affecting particular parts of the state more than others. Labour could move around in response to demand, as in the USA, while business could exploit large home markets. Even where there was decentralisation, theories of fiscal federalism and devolution argued that redistributive matters, notably welfare, should be assigned to the higher level, with the lower level concentrating on service provision (Oates 1999). The higher level, it was argued, could more easily mobilise resources for redistribution and insure against asymmetrical economic shocks. Social citizenship was predicated on a shared community and sense of identity. Governments of the left feared that conservative local governments would fail to meet their expectations of social spending. State-wide administrative systems were seen as more efficient that fragmented ones.

Received ideas about federalism (and its near relative, devolution) also evolved. Under classical or 'coordinate' federalism, each level had its own defined competences, exercised separately. In the 'cooperative' federalism of the welfare era, functions straddle all levels and governments worked together through elaborate systems of intergovernmental relations. Policy fields are integrated vertically rather than horizontally and policy communities straddle levels of government.

Since the 1970s, there has been a significant ideological shift in western countries away from the old Keynesian welfare formula. Keynesianism economic management was widely rejected, making only a brief comeback at the onset of the global financial crisis. It has proved more difficult in individual countries as, with free trade, the effects of any economic stimulus could leak away into other states. The EU itself has refused to adopt a continental-wide stimulus package in the face of recession and stagnation. Political support for welfare has declined in the face of new forms of poverty and precariousness. The welfare state, rather than being presented as a form of insurance and investment for everyone, is increasingly a divisive theme as political debate has reverted to distinctions between the deserving and undeserving poor. With the end of the full employment widely enjoyed in the Keynesian era, there has been a move from passive welfare benefits towards activation policies aimed at bringing people into the labour market. Focus has moved from the stable male-breadwinner-headed family towards a more complex conceptualisation of need and an appreciation of new risks including precarious employment and lack of skills.

Rescaling

At the same time as policy fields have been redefined, they are rescaling territorially, moving to new levels above and below the state (Keating 2013). The best-documented example concerns the economy. As the nation state is less able to define and manage a 'national economy', interest has shifted to the transnational scale but also to the sub-state regional level. There is now a large literature on the importance of the local and regional scale to the understanding of economic change and of the linkages of the local to the continental and global levels (Cooke and Morgan 1998; Scott 1998). Some of this is explained by traditional spatial location theory, referring to factors of production and proximity to natural resources, markets and transport nodes. The New Economic Geography (Krugman 2011) brought back considerations of space in the 1990s after a period of neglect in the economic mainstream. Alfred Marshall's (1920) work on industrial districts came back into fashion.

There are several variations of the 'new regionalism' in economic geography. Some stay close to classical economics in emphasising transaction costs and economies of agglomeration as the key to investment location. Other accounts are more institutionalist, focusing on the importance of institutions in government and civil society in promoting the conditions for successful enterprise. Emphasis has move away from the traded dependencies of transaction costs models to untraded interdependencies in the form of tacit knowledge and face-to-face exchange. It is this which explains why industries that might be prime candidates for territorialisation, like information technology or financial services, are so often spatially clustered. Institutional accounts fade into sociological accounts, focusing on the characteristics of local societies, including social capital and culture (Keating, Loughlin and Deschouwer 2003).

In the new regionalist literature, regions and localities are more than mere locations of productions but become production systems, with their own internal logic and interdependencies among themselves (Crouch et al. 2001). In another move, these systems are portrayed as being in competition as Ricardian comparative advantage (in which each unit has its place in the division of labour) gives way to absolute advantage (Scott

1998). This is a contentious point. Many economists would insist that only firms compete and that talking of regional competition merely reifies arbitrary spatial entities. The idea of interregional competition has, however, been taken up by territorial elites, who find it an attractive electoral theme, unifying their populations. It is also promoted by states and the European Commission as a model for economic development to supersede the old diversionary regional policies. The emphasis now is on endogenous development and what regions can do for themselves. Of course, logically it is impossible for all regions to become more competitive simultaneously, as it is a relative concept, but the theme has nonetheless become a powerful one, inspired by the work of Michael Porter (2001).

The diversionary regional policies of the Keynesian era have been run down. The opening of national economic borders through global and European free trade and capital mobility allows firms freely to shift their investment, so they cannot be forced to locate in developing regions. The old logic, by which transfers to poor regions came back to the wealthy regions as orders for their goods, no longer holds as consumers can spend their money on imports. Regional policy is expensive and less affective and is highly restricted by European competition policies.

There has also been some rescaling of welfare (Ferrera 2005; Kazepov and Barberis 2008). Poverty and deprivation have repeatedly been conceptualised as spatially concentrated, with their various dimensions causally linked. The new approaches, based on labour market activation, emphasise education and skills, which may be devolved (as in Scotland) and the need to connect welfare to labour markets, which are often regional and local. These in turn are linked to local and regional economic development initiatives. Consequently, welfare states have acquired important local, regional and transnational dimensions.

Moreover, the old distinctions between redistributive and allocative policies or between economic and social objectives are increasingly difficult to make since, as policy spheres restructure, all policies have a redistributive impact. Economic development can be presented as a positive-sum policy in the interests of the entire community but any given development strategy will always entail winners and losers. Education policy is both redistributive if financed by progressive taxation, and economic in that it improves the quality of the workforce. This is one reason why it is so tempting a field for politicians. New policies for social inclusion based on labour market activation are both social and economic. Public service reform, often sold as purely a matter of allocative efficiency, does have distributive effects (Pollitt and Bouckaert 2011). So as policy spheres are shifting both sectorally and spatially, social solidarity may continue to rest upon shared national identities but in plurinational states that identity itself is contested (McEwen and Moreno 2005). Scotland is not the only place where demands for national self-government have been linked to a relocation of the focus of solidarity from one nation to the other; it has been a major issue in Quebec (McEwen 2006; Béland and Lecours 2008). The assumption that social citizenship must be located at the level of the nation state has come under challenge, especially in plurinational states (Henderson et al. 2013).

Government has also been rescaling as a result both of top-down and bottom-up pressures. States have sought more effective levels of intervention and regulation. Political movements have demanded greater control over local and regional development priorities. Territory has been used as a basis for demands for social solidarity and welfare. Historic nations and regions have revived, with demands for self-government combining arguments for identity with those of the new regionalism. All the large states of Europe and some of the smaller ones now have an intermediate or 'meso' level of government between the central state and the localities.

Thinking about federalism and devolution has also shifted, from cooperative federalism and devolution to competitive federalism, moving away from integration and intergovernmental interdependence towards differentiation and competition. Devolved governments may compete for inward investment in line with the competitive regionalism model. They also compete in service provision, policy innovation, experimentation and differentiation. The vertical logic of traditional intergovernmental relations (between centre and periphery) may give way to horizontal links among territories. Rather than hierarchy, there may be scope for comparison and policy learning. Devolved governments are also open to European networks, variously competing and cooperating in European space and seeking to influence the policies of the EU.

It has often been assumed that there is a trade-off between

competitiveness and social cohesion in that market economies generate wealth but increase inequality. This dilemma would appear to be even more acute under conditions of competitive regionalism. Critics of decentralisation within states have evoked the danger of a 'race to the bottom' in social provision as regions compete to attract wealthy taxpayers and investors by cutting taxes. Neo-liberal commentators, for their part, have seen competition as providing necessary discipline (Ohmae 1995; Porter 2001; Alesina and Spolaore 2003).

The evidence on this is in fact mixed. There may indeed be a danger of a 'race to the bottom' but there are examples of competitive federalism and devolution encouraging a race to the top as regions compete to impress their electorates and to innovate (Gallego and Subirats 2011). Devolution in the UK has if anything produced a race to the top as the devolved administrations have sought to extend social entitlements and universalism, albeit subject to tight budgetary constraints. Devolved regions and nations are open territories, without the ability of the old nation state to contain social and economic systems and prevent partial exit, but they do have financial and policy instruments that might enable them to forge a distinct synthesis of economic and social policies to confront global challenges.

Scotland provides a stark example of all of these processes as new economic and social challenges map onto new spatial scales. A way out of these dilemmas and of resetting the terms of debate is the concept of social investment, which upon three strands presents formidable challenges.

Social investment

A first strand is to challenge the idea that growth and equality are, in a competitive market economy, mutually exclusive. There is now a strong body of thought to the effect that massive social inequality, far from stimulating development, is a hindrance to growth (Wilkinson and Pickett 2010; Stiglitz 2012; Ostry, Berg and Tsangarides 2014). A second strand is to question the assumption that public expenditure, especially on social support, is a hindrance to growth. While the market liberal approach to political economy sees low taxes and light regulation as the key to economic competitiveness, the social investment model (Crouch 2013; Hemerijck 2013) presents public expenditure not as a drain on the productive economy but as part of it. The issue is not whether expenditure is undertaken by the public or the private sector but what it is spent on. So education represents investment in human capital while health spending can enhance productivity. Research is a contribution to innovation and economic renewal. Expenditure on childcare allows mothers to remain in the labour market, so expanding the workforce and retaining skills. Investment in the early years contributes to economic prosperity, improving skills while reducing the later burden of social marginalisation. A third strand is the focus on 'preventive spending', meaning expenditure now, in order to reduce future outlay needs by anticipating and dealing with social problems in good time.

It is tempting to idealise the social investment model as a magic formula which enhances both economic competitiveness and social welfare, allowing us to escape with one bound from the crucial dilemma between growth and equity. In practice, matters are not so straightforward. Critics have claimed that 'social investment' may be just another 'Third Way' attempt to square circles or a way to justify public services at a time of financial constraint and neo-liberal hegemony. It may subordinate social justice and equality to the economy, thus accepting the premises of neo-liberalism if not its conclusions. By focusing on productive labour, the social investment approach might favour the better-off members of society or those who could most easily be brought into the workforce (Rhodes 2013). There is a broad consensus that the most effective way of tackling deprivation and other social problems is to get people into work, but sharp differences on how this might be achieved. While neo-liberals favour punitive approaches to unemployment, by reducing welfare benefits and imposing strict requirements, the social democratic social investment approach privileges preparation. It is also important to note that the old social risks, principally of cyclical unemployment, have not gone away. So no amount of preparation and job training is going to get people into work if there are not enough jobs to go around. It can merely allow politicians to blame the unemployed for their own condition. Preventive spending is also a difficult concept in practice and can easily be used as a slogan to justify any item of spending that an actor wants to prioritise.

The ideas of social investment and preventive spending have become very fashionable in government and feature prominently in the discourse of Scottish politicians. They are, however, extremely difficult to operationalise and to sustain. It is necessary to identify which expenditures are efficiency-enhancing and contribute to economic growth. They also require that a society have the capacity and political will to postpone gratification in the present for future gain, and to take account of the needs of future generations. This requires that the right instruments and institutions be available in government, the economy and civil society.

Policy instruments

If we compare them with independent states the instruments available to devolved governments to face these huge challenges appear rather weak. They lack control of significant macro-economic levers, which states retain in in the form of spending, taxation and (outside the Euro zone) monetary policy. The Scottish Government's overall tax powers are now substantial but it operates within a balanced budget constraint, with borrowing powers limited to those needed for large capital projects and short-term bridging to deal with fluctuating revenue streams. This largely precludes the use of taxation and spending to deliver an economic stimulus on Keynesian lines (and so curtails its ability to counter 'austerity').

With a few exceptions (notably the Basque Country), devolved governments in Europe have few powers of taxation of business (and those limited mostly to property taxes). The SNP has demanded the devolution of corporation tax with a view to cutting it as an incentive to inward investors but this has been refused (although conceded to Northern Ireland). Scotland does have control over regional development grants, another instrument to attract inward investment, but these are subject to UK and European rules about eligibility and levels. On the other hand, devolved governments, including Scotland, can use interventions at the micro-level as well as supply-side instruments such as education training, infrastructure and research and development. The new theories suggest that these can be very significant.

Compared with other devolved legislatures in Europe, the Scottish Parliament has very extensive scope for law-making, since only the reserved powers are specified and everything else is devolved. Unlike many other countries, the UK lacks extensive framework laws within which the devolved legislatures must work. This permits extensive innovation in the design of policy and the relationship among policy fields. On the other hand, many of the issues with which we are concerned are less amenable to legislative solutions but concern detailed policy design and delivery. Legislation can set the framework for policy but, if it becomes too detailed, can stifle innovation and flexibility.

The Scottish Government possesses significant regulatory powers, for example in land use, but much regulation is reserved to Westminster or to the EU. Scotland has few powers over competition or monopolies and its economic policies are hitherto subject to European regulations, which restrict the extent of intervention allowed.

The Scottish Parliament is responsible for a substantial budget, accounting for some 60 per cent of public spending in Scotland and rising by around another 5 per cent after the Scotland Act (2016). Hitherto it has received nearly all of this from Westminster and passed around two-thirds of this on, mainly to local government and the National Health Service. This left limited room for policy change at the Scottish level. With the 2016 Act, the Scottish Parliament will now receive just over half of its revenues from its own sources, allowing it greater scope on the revenue side, while still passing on the greater part of it. This includes a share of VAT, which it has no power to change but which could provide an incentive to stimulate economic growth. The proportion of its income from the taxes it does control is a little under 40 per cent.

The main discretionary tax is income tax (amounting to some 70 per cent of the discretionary tax). As the Scottish Parliament will be able to set the income tax bands, it can make taxes more progressive, charging high earners more in order to reduce inequality. On the other hand, Scotland will not control the definition of income or taxes on unearned income. Income tax is a highly visible imposition and politically difficult to raise – the basic rate has never been raised since the 1970s but only cut. In a competitive environment, there is the risk that any effort to increase income tax, especially on the rich and mobile, could be self-defeating as people might move out, at least for fiscal purposes, or transform earned income into dividends or capital gains.

The new welfare powers that Scotland has acquired under the Scotland Act (2016) include discretionary housing payments, attendance allowance, disability living allowance, carer's allowance, industrial injuries benefits, severe disablement allowance and winter fuel payments. On the other hand, all the benefits that were due to be incorporated into Universal Credit under the UK Government's welfare reform were ruled out for devolution. This includes most measures of income support for the poor and unemployed, which have the most immediate effect on income inequalities. There is a power to top up reserved benefits, which looks like a powerful tool but this would require additional expenditure. The Scottish Parliament does not therefore have the ability to design its own welfare settlement by replacing UK benefits with its own. The administration of the Work Programme, the main welfare-to-work instrument, was devolved but not the design of the programme itself. So the Scottish Parliament cannot design its own set of incentives and penalties in order to link active labour market policies to welfare entitlement.

A potential benefit of devolution is that territorial governments can redefine policy problems, link previously disparate policy fields and bring resources to bear more effectively. This depends on having a policy capacity (Pasquier 2004) in the sense of the ability to analyse policy issues and devise responses. The Scottish Government is the descendant of the old Scottish Office, which was not primarily a policy-making department but rather adapted polices set at the centre (Midwinter, Keating and Mitchell 1991). In the years following devolution, Labour-led administrations were in office at both Scottish and UK levels, following broadly similar policy lines, with the main difference being that Scotland did not always follow the UK on the agenda of contracting out and marketisation in the public sector (Keating 2010). There was also a generous financial settlement, so that Scotland never had to use the limited tax powers it had (the ability to raise or lower income tax by up to three pence in the pound) or to make hard spending choices. Broad policy lines were agreed by the two coalition parties (Labour and Liberal Democrat) at the start of each session, leaving less room for policy innovation in between.

The arrival of the SNP in government in 2007 was followed by a reorganisation of government with the aim of focusing better on policy objectives. Departments were abolished in favour of directorates organised around policy themes and a less hierarchical arrangement in which civil servants at a relatively low level could interact directly with ministers. A National Performance Framework was introduced with a hierarchy of policy aims and objectives. This gave a greater strategic sense to government (civil servants for a time would carry around laminated versions of the Performance Framework) but it is usually difficult to work out exactly what difference mechanisms like this make to day-to-day decisions. The budgetary process continued to revolve around negotiations among ministers in charge of spending programmes rather than the strategic objectives and priorities.

Effective government also depends critically on political will and courage. Scottish governments since devolution have been risk-averse, which may be the counterpart of the search for consensus within policy communities. The incoming SNP government in 2007 made some important decisions, for example on university fees and some minor gestures like the abolition of tolls on the estuarial bridges but after 2011 was preoccupied with the proposed referendum. The subsequent campaign was marked by further risk-aversion and a reluctance on the part of both sides to face up to difficult policy choices. The pro-independence side held up the Nordic countries as models of small independent nations that combined economic success with high social cohesion and relatively low levels of inequality. The SNP (if not the left-wing independence movements), however, was reluctant to face up to the corollary, that a Nordic welfare state implies higher levels of taxation. The election campaign of 2016, the first held under the new provisions for tax-raising powers, followed similar lines. The SNP, Labour and the Liberal Democrats all proposed tax levels that would be higher than those prevailing in England but only slightly. So Labour and the Liberal Democrats proposed a penny on the standard and higher rates of taxation, while the SNP promised not to pass on the whole of the rise in the threshold for the higher rate introduced in the UK budget of 2016.

Successive Scottish governments have tended to pursue a more universalist form of service provision than in England, including such matters as free undergraduate university tuition, abolition of prescription charges and broader coverage of personal care for the elderly (Keating 2010). There is a long argument in social policy as to whether universal or selective provision of free services is more socially egalitarian. On the one hand, it is argued that free university tuition benefits the middle classes at the expense of working-class families whose children are less likely to go to university. Free personal care, when it was introduced by the Labour/Liberal Democrat administration was criticised for favouring wealthy elderly people who could afford to pay (although the same might be said of the entire health service). On the other hand, it is argued that services free at the point of use help to create social solidarity and tie the middle classes into the welfare state. This is a key feature of the Nordic model but does imply high levels of taxation.

Policy constraints

Within its reserved powers, the Scottish Government and Parliament are constrained by two sets of forces. First is the intergovernmental system. Although the division of competences between Edinburgh and London is, compared with other systems, reasonably clear, there are still overlaps and shared responsibilities, for example in economic development. This area of shared competence is now being extended with the devolution of welfare powers, which are linked in multiple ways to UK policy instruments. In systems of cooperative federalism, as in Germany, much policy is made in the intergovernmental arena, with the lower level responsible for administration. This is not the spirit behind Scottish devolution, which is aimed at allowing policy divergence and diversity. Intergovernmental relations since devolution have been rather informal and ad hoc. There have been repeated calls to make them more formal and institutionalised, giving the devolved administrations a stronger voice at the centre. Students of federalism have pointed to two aspects: self-rule in the form of autonomous policy making; and shared rule, meaning influence of the lower level at the centre. There is a dilemma here, as the more Scotland is tied into inter-governmental networks, the less autonomy it has to design its own policies.

The intergovernmental networks have included the European Union, whose competences cover both reserved and devolved matters. European competition policies reach down to the devolved and local levels and constrain the ability of governments to intervene in markets or to subsidise economic activities.

Europe is also a source of policy innovation and support, especially in matters of economic development and social progress. Scotland has been able to influence European Union policies through the UK Government, which consults with devolved governments through the Joint Ministerial Committee. UK withdrawal from the European Union will remove European constraints but we do not know what UK-wide mechanisms may replace them in competition policy or state aids. During the Brexit referendum, the Scottish Government supported not only continuing membership but the idea of the 'European social model' of the economy and welfare state, in line with its own preferences for linking the economic with the social. If the UK is to compete in the wider global market without the European framework, it may be more difficult to retain this model in the face of pressures to cut costs and social overheads. Alternatively, Scotland may choose to become independent, looking more to the European Union than the UK.

The second constraint on policy making is provided by the open border with the rest of the UK and (hitherto) the EU and the economic pressures this creates. There is a fear that if Scotland raises taxes or imposes too many extra regulations, businesses and wealthy people will move out. This was the reason given by the SNP in 2016 for abandoning its previous proposal to raise the highest marginal rate of income tax from 45 to 50 per cent. Were Scotland to raise benefits and service levels substantially, there is a possibility that people could move in to take advantage, although there is limited international evidence for 'welfare tourism' in devolved systems. The Smith Commission proposed that, if one government took action that imposed a cost (or 'detriment') on the other, then compensation might be payable. This was soon abandoned as unworkable, but Scotland and England can certainly each be affected by decisions taken in the other jurisdiction. The SNP's policy of reducing and then abolishing Air Passenger Duty could divert traffic from other UK airports, especially in the north of England, which would not be well received in England and could spark a race to the bottom. This is the main reason why corporation tax was not devolved and, if it were, there could be a similar race to cut it, with consequent losses of public revenues.

Social partnership

One way in which small nations have sought to overcome these vulnerabilities and manage the terms of their relationship with the outside world is through social partnership or concertation. In the 1980s, Katzenstein (1985) identified the secret of adaptation of small states to global markets as corporatism, a mode of policy making in which government, business and trade unions thrash out positive-sum agreements on long-term goals and commitments (Schmitter 1974). Unions can accept wage restraint and thus contain inflation and business costs, in return for full employment and increases in real wages. They may accept lower individual wage increases in return for increases in the 'social wage' in the form of public services such as health and education, which directly benefit their members. Business commits to investment in the knowledge that markets will expand, wages will be under control and infrastructure provided. Government agrees to fund public services and expand infrastructure, in the knowledge that the other partners will deliver their part of the bargain. The UK made sporadic efforts at corporatism in the 1960s and 1970s but these foundered on the inability of the three partners to deliver on their commitments.

Corporatism generally was in decline by the 1980s, as a result of globalisation and the opening of markets. In the 1990s, however, in an effort to regain competitiveness and to qualify for the single European currency, a number of European states adopted 'lean corporatism' (Rhodes 2001; Traxler 2004), 'social concertation' (Compston 2002), 'social pacts' (Avdagic, Rhodes and Visser 2011), 'social dialogue' or 'social partnership'. The European Commission was keen on the idea, buying into the idea of the social investment state and the new economic theories that emphasise human capital, research and entrepreneurship. Wage negotiation often remained at the core of these bargains. Training and active labour market policy are key ingredients, linked to competitiveness. Partnership is sometimes extended beyond capital and labour to social interests, the voluntary sector and environmentalists.

Social partnership has been tried at the sub-state level but faces particular difficulties (Keating 2013; Keating and Wilson 2014). The social partners are not always organised there, or may be poorly resourced. Regions are weakly bounded spaces so that actors, notably business, can exit easily and so are not bound into social compromises. Wage bargaining remains at national or, increasingly, plant level, so removing a central element of the bargain, the ability to trade off the wages at work with the social wage. The main taxation powers remain at the centre, which reduces the incentive of social partners to invest in regional or local concertation. That said, devolved governments have sought to incorporate the social partners through a variety of mechanisms, including social and economic councils (in France), formal concertation (in Italy) and regionalism-level reproduction of corporatist negotiations (in Belgium) (Keating and Wilson 2014).

There was a territorial element in British corporatism in the 1960s and 1970s. The Labour Government's National Plan of 1965 was accompanied by regional plans and Economic Development Councils were set up in the nations and regions. The English councils were closed down by the incoming Conservative Government in 1979; the Scottish Economic Council survived for a few years longer. At the time of devolution to Scotland interest in social partnership revived, with particular focus on the Irish model (which itself crashed in the financial crisis of 2008). Partnership remains central to the Scottish Government's policy model, with its emphasis on the inclusion of 'stakeholders'. Trade unions have continued to advocate it and there is a concordat with the Scottish Trades Union Congress (STUC). STUC now supports devolution of labour market policies and industrial relations to Scotland, where it feels that trade unions would have better access. There is a National Economic Forum but it lacks the research and policy capacity of similar bodies in other countries and is more of a sounding board.

The preconditions for corporatism or concerted action are not, however, obvious in Scotland. Sociologists have drawn attention to different models of capitalism (Hall and Soskice 2001). In liberal market economies, firms compete individually, aiming to maximise profits and share value in the short term. In coordinated market economies, business is organised in associations, which regulate their own affairs and cooperate (as well as competing) to produce public goods from which they can all benefit. Firms look to the long term and aim at increasing market share and expanding production, rather than maximising profit in the short term. Such firms are more likely to be amenable to corporatist bargaining and collective action, especially when they are domestically owned.

Another condition is strong and centralised associations representing business and labour, which can come to agreements and deliver them. If business firms can opt out, they can free ride by enjoying the benefits without paying the dues. If trade unions do not cover the work force, they similarly will be unable to deliver. The broader the coverage of unions, moreover, the more they overlap with society and so have an incentive to focus on the social wage rather than just the sectoral interests of their own members.

Scotland, like the rest of the UK, is a liberal market economy. Trade unions are mostly UK-wide and not subject to policy direction from the STUC. The middle-sized tier of business is weak in Scotland, and the Scottish business class declined with the reduction of domestic ownership from the First World War. Employers' bodies are UK-wide, have relatively weak Scottish structures, do not speak for a united business interest, and are not interested in social partnership. The SNP proposal in its independence White Paper (Scottish Government 2013) to cut corporation tax to three pence less than the UK rate, is indicative of the state of affairs. In a concerted action system or social partnership, this is the kind of concession that might have been granted in return for action on the part of business rather than extended to all business without asking for anything in return. Nor is Scotland a unit for wage bargaining, except in some parts of the public sector, so there is limited capacity to trade off wages against the social wage. On the other hand the increased taxation powers under the Scotland Acts of 2012 and 2016 might provide incentives for the main economic groups to strengthen their Scottish structures and think more deeply about the need to balance tax-raising with expenditure.

Successive Scottish governments have instead put the emphasis on including social partners (or 'stakeholders') in policy subfields. In 2015–16 there was a series of national conversations around themes of social justice and health. This has become almost a defining feature of the Scottish policy model (Keating 2010). It might be considered a form of sectoral partnership or corporatism, building on the large degree of consensus that prevails in many sectors and, in some areas like education, using policy communities that existed before devolution. What is missing is the ability to work across traditional policy communities and a forum in which social compromises can be worked out, for example between business-led ideas about economic development, social priorities and environmental concerns. Instead, successive governments have been committed to a policy programme focused primarily on economic development on the assumption that other desired goals will follow.

Public opinion

In recent decades, Scotland has been discursively constructed as a more caring and egalitarian society than that of England; this was a strong theme in the referendum campaign. Yet surveys have consistently shown that on measures of support for redistribution, Scottish voters are only marginally to the left of England. This would seem to impose a severe constraint on policy innovation and action on inequalities and explains the reluctance of the political parties to make more radical proposals at election time. To stop the argument there, however, would be misleading. Redistributive policies do not come about because individuals altruistically desire to give away some of their income and wealth to others. They happen within particular social and institutional contexts in which citizens see a connection between the common good and their own individual interest (Rothstein and Steinmo 2013). This is part of a broader social bargain, which is strengthened in turn where citizens trust government to act responsibly and in the public interest. It is also the case that citizen preferences may follow rather than precede government policies, as long as they value the services they are getting. This is the basis upon which the scope of government expanded so radically during the twentieth century and has been identified as a key element in support for the social democratic settlement in Scandinavia (Rothstein and Steino 2013). Whether Scotland could generate and sustain such a settlement is an open question.

The chapters

The broad aim of this book is to explore the scope that Scotland has to achieve the proclaimed goals of economic growth and a reduction of social inequalities through the use of its existing and new powers. This includes a shift to social investment and prevention and a new positive-sum social compromise. The following chapters of this book explore these issues in more detail in key policy fields.

Patrizio Lecca, Peter McGregor and Kim Swales examine the tax powers of the Scottish Parliament including the new income tax powers, the assigned VAT revenues and the possible devolution of corporation tax. As Scotland still has only minor borrowing powers, they model 'balanced budget' changes in which spending increases must be covered by taxation. In their first scenario, spending and taxes are both increased, which provokes demands for compensatory wage increases and a decline in competitiveness of Scottish firms. In the second scenario, increased services attract incoming workers. Workers in general appreciate the services as part of the 'social wage' offsetting reductions in private incomes through tax increases and so do not press for compensating wage increases. In the third scenario, the increased expenditure serves as social investment, which increases growth. Which of these happens will depend on how far the public values increased services, on wage bargaining behavior, and on the positive economic effects of public spending. These last might be through capital spending or the wider effects of social investment.

Corporation tax is not currently devolved but its devolution has been suggested as a tool for economic promotion. In Lecca, McGregor and Swales' model, cutting corporation tax does stimulate growth but this could be negated if there was a corresponding increase in income tax. That could, moreover, provoke wage demands, further reducing competitiveness. The social wage would also fall. In the long run, growth could be enhanced if lower taxes attracted more inward direct investment but only if other jurisdictions did not retaliate with their own reductions.

The devolution and assignment of taxes may have other effects as Scotland depends more on its own revenues, giving it an incentive to pursue pro-growth policies. In the long term, the outcome also depends on the new block grant mechanisms and Scotland's demographics. The Scottish economy remains closely linked to the wider UK economy and changes in one will continue to have spill-over effects into the other. Much also depends on institutions, for example the existence or absence of a Scottish level of collective bargaining so that wage increases can take account of Scottish conditions and private wages adjusted to recognise increases in the social wage.

David Bell, David Eiser and Katerina Lisenkova address the question of inequality. Inequality has been rising across the western world and is increasingly seen as both a social and an economic problem. Three drivers have been identified. The first is globalisation and economic change, which enhance the chances of those with portable skills. The second is the tendency for the return to capital to increase faster than the economy itself. The third is increases in asset prices, such as property, which are not linked to productive output. There is inequality within each age group and, of increasing interest, between age groups and past and future generations.

Governments have a number of instruments to combat inequality: taxes; unemployment and welfare benefits; regulation; labour market and collective bargaining policy; and universal public services including education and health. Some policies, on the other hand, work to increase inequality; this is the case of the Quantitative Easing monetary policy adopted in the wake of the global financial crisis. Sub-state governments possess only some of these powers. They control taxes but raising these could provoke a flight of firms and wealthy individuals. On the other hand, public services can be used in the long term to enhance human capital and chances in the labour market.

Inequality in Scotland is slightly lower than the UK average, but mainly because of the concentration of the wealthy in London. Intergenerational inequality is rather more severe. The Scottish Government has limited influence over these patterns and more progressive income taxes could be counter-productive if they drove away the higher earning 1 per cent who pay 20 per cent of the income tax. Longer-term measures focused on human capital would be more promising.

Nicola McEwen examines the new social security powers under the Scotland Act of 2016. Scotland already had substantial powers over the delivery of public services but the new powers affect cash payments as well. Some 15 per cent of social security spending is now devolved. There is some flexibility in the delivery of the Universal Credit, which itself remains reserved. There is also a power to create new benefits and top up reserved benefits. There has already been a change in emphasis as the term 'social security' has been reintroduced as a less stigmatising substitute for 'welfare'. After some debate, the Scottish Government decided to establish its own delivery agency rather than using the Department of Work and Pensions machinery. This brings the promises of more user-friendly delivery.

On the other hand, Scotland's scope for introducing a radically different system is constrained. It cannot abolish existing reserved benefits so that any new ones will be an added expense at a time of fiscal restraint. Many of the devolved benefits are for elderly people, who place growing demands on the system, while the new fiscal framework does not fully compensate for this, leaving Scotland with the risk; this is the counterpart to getting more tax powers. The 'no detriment' principle from the Smith Commission is still to be worked out in practice but aims to provide for compensation if the act of one government imposes a cost on the other. There are complex interconnections as some benefits are 'passported', in the sense that eligibility for one is the criterion for eligibility for others; sometimes these belong to two governments. There is some devolution of active labour market policies, but this does not include unemployment allowances so precluding a new approach to linking labour markets to the benefits system.

Scotland can therefore take some action towards creating a more egalitarian welfare system but it will still remain embedded in a wider UK economy, labour market and welfare state.

Craig McAngus and Kirstein Rummery examine childcare. This has been widely promoted as a policy that meets social and economic targets at the same time. It can enhance gender equality by improving women's opportunities in the labour market and, by providing subsidised universal coverage, benefit lower-income families. At the same time, by bringing more women into the labour market it can increase the labour force and add to economic growth, possibly even to the point of paying for itself. It is an important component of the Nordic welfare mix. Hitherto, childcare in Scotland has largely been market-based and demand- rather than supply-driven, but the SNP Government have large ambitions, which featured in the referendum debate. Scotland has always had competence in this field but hitherto the tax revenues that might be generated from increased labour force participation have gone to the UK Treasury. Now the income taxes will come to the Scottish Government.

On the other hand, parental leave and most welfare policies

are a reserved matter and these are a key component of family policies in other jurisdictions. This balance might be changed with further devolution or flexibility in applying UK policies, as happens in Quebec's successful system. Germany also shows how differentiated policies are possible in a federal system.

Paul Cairney, Malcolm Harvey and Emily St Denny look at the capacity of the Scottish Government to move towards a policy stance based on social investment and prevention. They are critical of the lack of clarity with which these concepts have been defined. They appear unexceptionable but are notoriously difficult to apply and, indeed, almost any policy can potentially be so labelled. The Scottish Government was committed to them and they did feature in the SNP's independence prospectus, as part of a distinct small-state or Nordic approach to policy but only gradually is this being worked out. The policy streams literature suggests that change requires an identifiable problem, an available policy and a political opportunity. The independence referendum might have provided a window of opportunities to apply new approaches to policy making, but the definition of the problem and the solution were too vague.

Scotland, moreover, lacks the preconditions for a Nordic-type approach to policy, including social partnership, support for welfare, acceptance of a universalist approach and strong social solidarity. The Scottish Government claims a distinct approach to policy making but this differs significantly from those in the Nordic states in the degree of incorporation of social interests and the strength of the social partners. Under the devolution settlement, Scottish priorities may differ from those at the UK level. On the other side, much of the implementation is down to local government and agencies. In a more limited way, however, the Scottish Government has experimented with new approaches in evidence-based medicine, storytelling approaches and collaborative methods.

Michael Keating and Robert Liñeira examine public support for more solidaristic and redistributive policies in Scotland. They find that Scots are, at best, only slightly more inclined to redistribution than citizens in the rest of the UK. Like those elsewhere, they might be persuaded to pay higher taxes if these were hypothecated to health and, perhaps, education but are reluctant to spend more on welfare. Moreover, support for redistribution has been declining over recent years.

This, however, is a static view of attitudes. There is evidence that public preferences may follow rather than precede policies so that there is scope for leadership. Preferences also need to be seen as part of a wider social compromise so that citizens will support taxation if they can be assured that the money will be well spent and that their individual interest and the broader social interest coincide. The question is then whether Scotland, with its present balance of competences, can generate this form of enlightened self-interest.

The new devolution settlement does allow decisions on taxes and spending to be taken in the same place and for trade-offs to be made. On the other hand, the chapters in the book have shown how the balance of competences may not facilitate this kind of social compromise. The progressivity of the tax system is limited by the difficulties of taxing mobile high earners and the reservation of taxes on unearned income and business. The reservation of most welfare benefits means that the Scottish Government can only complement them or top them up, rather than designing its own system. The reservation of labour market policy makes it difficult to link this to welfare or to promote trade union membership. The continued existence of UK-wide or firm-level collective bargaining makes it difficult to incorporate a Scottish social wage into bargaining so allowing a different mix between private and public consumption.

There are opportunities in the new powers to create a wealthier and fairer Scotland but they are constrained. Of course, under independence there would also be constraints on policy choices but the chapters of this book suggest that the present balance of powers, which was, as we know, the result of an essentially political compromise in the weeks following the independence referendum, may need to addressed again if Scotland is to find its own combination of economic dynamism and social cohesion.

2 Taxes and Spending

*Patrizio Lecca, Peter G. McGregor and Kim Swales**

Introduction

The outcome of the referendum on Scottish independence held on 18 September 2014 implies that Scotland remains a member of the UK for the foreseeable future. However, while complete fiscal autonomy is ruled out for now, significant changes in the Scottish fiscal system have occurred since the referendum. First, some tax changes embodied in the Scotland Act, 2012 were implemented in April 2015 and 2016. Second, further tax powers were devolved under the Scotland Act 2016. Third, a new fiscal framework for the Scottish Government was agreed, with a new formula for calculating the block grant from Westminster in the light of the new tax powers.

In this chapter, we briefly review the tax and spending powers introduced by the Scotland Acts of 2012 and 2016. We consider each of these changes in turn and seek to identify those that have the potential to exert significant macroeconomic or system-wide effects on the Scottish economy. Then we provide a first attempt to analyse the likely consequences of changes in those taxes that either are devolved, or could be devolved in future, and that could exert a significant system-wide impact on the Scottish economy. While there has been extensive debate around the issue of which powers should be devolved, there has been much less consideration of how these powers should be used, and their likely impacts on the Scottish economy.

We then reflect on the wider lessons of our analysis for two key aspects of the debate on further devolution of fiscal powers: the link between Scottish economic activity and Scottish

Government revenues; and fairness, well-being and inequality in Scotland. The conclusion outlines the further research that would enable us better to understand Scotland's future fiscal choices and their likely consequences.

Fiscal powers for the Scottish Parliament

When the Scottish Parliament was established in 1999, its spending powers were wide but its taxation powers very limited. The most important was the ability to raise or lower the rate on income tax by one percentage point, a power that was never actually used. Important changes were introduced in the Scotland Act (2012) (and implemented in April 2015 and 2016) and in the Scotland Act (2016).[1]

The Scottish Land and Buildings Transactions Tax (LBTT) and the Scottish Landfill Tax both came into effect in April 2015. The former replaced the UK Stamp Duty Land Tax by a progressive tax that avoids the distortions created by the slab tax, in which tax liabilities increased sharply as property values exceeded certain thresholds. While this seems a more efficient and, given its progressivity (and tougher tax avoidance provisions), a fairer tax, its introduction on a revenue-neutral basis makes it inevitable that reducing the burden on lower property values, as the Scottish Government intends, will increase the tax burden on higher valued properties.[2] The Scottish Landfill Tax replaces its UK counterpart, and has the attraction of covering illegal landfilling and providing greater incentives to stimulate community action. While both changes are welcome, each accounts for a very modest proportion of total tax revenue in Scotland, and so is unlikely to have any meaningful macroeconomic impact.

By far the most significant changes are those to income taxation. The Scotland Act of 2012 devolved half of income tax to Scotland but this was overtaken by the Scotland Act of 2016, which devolved all of income tax (bands and rates) on non-savings and non-dividend income in Scotland, which accounts for 23 per cent of total tax revenue, from April 2017. This provides the Scottish Government with very considerable powers over income taxation, including the degree of progressivity. The objective of the devolved tax powers is to make the Scottish Government have greater responsibility for its own expenditure decisions, with the share of revenues being raised in Scotland rising from 15 per cent to around one-third.

The devolution of taxes means that the block grant from the UK to the Scottish Parliament must be reduced accordingly. This is called the Block Grant Adjustment (BGA). The chosen approach to implement the 2012 Act was originally the indexed deduction (ID) method, in which a base year adjustment is calculated on expected tax revenues so that revenues of the Scottish Government would be maintained by keeping the Scottish income tax rate at 10 per cent (if actual revenues were equal to those expected). Subsequently, Scottish Government tax revenues will be indexed to comparable UK tax receipts, although under the Fiscal Framework agreed in 2016, an indexed per capita (IPC) method is to be used for the first five years. This was a victory for Scotland in that it at least partially insulates the Scottish Government's revenues from UK-wide changes, including recession and UK tax changes, since these impact on UK-wide revenues too, and there would be no adjustment if Scotland and RUK (the rest of the UK) were not differentially impacted by the change. However, Scottish-specific changes that result in higher revenues will result in an adjustment that grows less rapidly than tax revenues, providing an incentive to the Scottish Government to adopt growth-promoting policies.[3] The IPC does ensure that the Scottish Government's overall level of funding is unaffected if Scotland's population grows differently from RUK.

VAT accounts for the next highest share of tax revenues in Scotland (20 per cent), but EU law is judged to prevent the devolution of this tax. The Scotland Act assigns 50 per cent of Scottish revenues from VAT to the Scottish Parliament from 2019–20,which means that its revenues will depend on the level of economic activity generating VAT but it has no means of increasing the rate to make up any shortfall.

There was no agreement to devolve National Insurance contributions (18 per cent of Scottish tax revenues), although if these revenues are ultimately linked to income tax, as some have suggested, there may be a case for revisiting this in the future.[4] Nor was there widespread support for devolution of (onshore) corporation tax (6 per cent of Scottish tax revenues) to complement and underpin economic development, which is currently a devolved matter. There was, on the contrary, considerable opposition from business and political parties other than the SNP on the grounds of likely unproductive tax competition with RUK. The devolution of Air Passenger Duty (APD) received widespread support and is devolved from April 2018. Land value taxation and land site taxation are already devolved under the Scotland Act (2012), but these are small taxes that are unlikely to have system-wide ramifications.

The Scotland Act (2016) allows higher levels of devolution than in any other European country apart from the Basque and Navarre regions of Spain (Bell and Eiser 2014b). This is despite the fact that some of the other regions of the UK operate with a relatively low degree of autonomy. An already asymmetric devolved system will become even more so. However, such asymmetry could allow interesting assessment of the 'laboratory' argument in favour of fiscal federalism that permitting innovation in policy-setting in devolved regions may serve to reveal better policies that can be emulated by others or problematic policies that can be avoided by others.

Under the Scotland Act (2012), the Scottish Government could borrow up to £2.2 billion to finance capital investment via the National Loans Fund, commercial loans and, since February 2014, by issuing its own bonds. Under the Scotland Act (2016) the statutory limit on borrowing for capital spend is increased to £3 billion (with the annual cap raised to £450 million a year).

There has been extensive public discussion of which powers to devolve but much less about what a future Scottish Government should actually do with them. Past experience suggested that Scottish Governments might be reluctant to use their new powers. Successive administrations chose not to use the Scottish Variable Rate of three pence in the pound – indeed committed publicly to *not* using it – and it ultimately fell into disuse due to a failure to continue to pay for the maintenance of the tax base. Furthermore, none of the parties in the referendum debate made pledges radically to alter the mix of taxes and expenditures. The only party that committed to tax changes was the SNP, and it committed to *reductions* in corporation tax and APD, on the basis that these changes were likely ultimately to be self-funding by boosting economic activity. Similarly, the SNP made commitments to benefits, but to *maintaining* or *enhancing* them.[5] The Scotland Acts of 2012 and 2016, however, *require* the Scottish Parliament to set a Scottish rate of income tax (SRIT) so that inaction on income tax is no longer an option. However,

it always has the choice to act so as to maintain parity with
RUK income tax rates and, indeed, this was the outcome of the
first SRIT.

Some interesting differences on income tax began to emerge
during the 2016 election campaign for the Scottish Parliament.
Only the Conservatives committed to maintaining parity with
tax rates and allowances in the rest of the UK. The SNP dropped
their previous proposal of a rise in the highest rate of income
tax, given their judgement that this would drive away sufficient
numbers of taxpayers in this category to generate an actual
decline in tax revenue. They were also unwilling to raise standard rates because this would impact on some lower-income
groups. Instead, it committed to not matching the Conservative
UK Government's increase in the thresholds at which the forty
pence rate will be levied. The Labour Party proposed to raise
the basic and higher rates by one pence in the pound, and the
highest rate from forty-five pence to fifty pence in the pound,
while claiming that people on lower incomes would be pro-
tected by the increase in the personal allowance introduced in
the UK April budget (the personal allowance is not devolved).
The Green Party wished to increase the progressivity of the
income tax system significantly, with a sixty pence top rate and
new rate of forty-three pence (from £43,000).

In this chapter we explore the likely consequences of the
Scottish Government both possessing *and choosing to activate*
changes in a variety of taxes that are likely to exert a macroeconomic impact. Clearly, it would be wise for the Scottish
Government to anticipate the likely consequences of such
changes. Scotland will remain a small, highly open economy,
given the continued integration of Scottish and RUK labour and
capital markets. Policy choices will inevitably be constrained
by their anticipated (and actual) impacts. Nevertheless, post
Scotland Act (2016) there is considerable scope to alter the
levels of both government expenditure and taxes. This is not,
of course, a technical economic matter, but involves a fundamental political choice about the nature of the society in
which Scottish voters wish to live. For example, major tax and
expenditure increases would shift Scotland in the direction of
the Nordic countries, which have often been referred to as an
example for Scotland.

Significant reductions in tax rates and expenditures, on
the other hand, would move us in the direction of the Baltic

economies. Keating and Harvey (2014) characterise this as a choice between *social investment* and *market liberal* strategies, noting the attraction of the former in the Scottish context. In the social investment strategy, public expenditure is seen as a contribution to the productive economy rather than a drain on it. However, this does depend on the precise nature of public expenditure and how it is valued by residents of the host economy, aspects we begin to explore below.

While the mainstream parties in Scotland are now advocating different income tax policies, most advocate only modest changes. The Scotland Acts undoubtedly create the potential for radical change but there remain significant constraints on the Scottish Government's ability to vary the aggregate fiscal stance. There is some extension of borrowing powers. The Scottish Government is free to pursue balanced budget fiscal changes that do not impact on the overall fiscal stance; that is, they do not increase the deficit or debt. While revenues and expenditures have to move in the same direction, there is scope for significant shifts in the levels of both and in either direction.

To indicate the kind of considerations that a Scottish Government will have to weigh when anticipating the use of their new fiscal powers, we conduct a number of illustrative fiscal policy simulations in the next section of the chapter. These relate to the power to alter income tax rates, which has been significantly extended by the most recent Scotland Act. Although the Scottish Government will not have the power to change corporation tax rates in the near future, this continues to be advocated by some, and it is instructive to explore its potential impacts.

Under the Scotland Act (2016), the Scottish Government gains new powers over welfare benefits, with more discretion on their use (Chapter 4). These could potentially have economic effects in altering work incentives but there are currently no proposals for radical changes.[6] So we simplify our analysis, and focus on the potential impacts of balanced budget tax changes that are not used to alter the level of welfare benefits.

Scottish fiscal choices after the Scotland Act (2016)

First, we consider the impact of a balanced budget increase in income tax. For simplicity, we assume a three pence change in income tax, which would have been possible under all three of the tax systems that have been in place successively since 1999.

Second, we analyse the impact of a balanced budget reduction in corporation tax. This is not currently allowed but is some proposed by the SNP and is being extended to Northern Ireland. While economic theory can help inform us of the likely effects of such policies, there are often countervailing forces generated in response to tax and expenditure changes, with some tending to increase economic activity (the demand-stimulating effect of expenditure expansions) and others tending to reduce it (the supply-contracting effects of rises in income tax rates). Often, economic theory alone is incapable of identifying even the direction of change that would be likely to result from a particular policy change.

We explore these policy changes by performing simulations using AMOS, a computable general equilibrium model of the Scottish economy (Harrigan et al. 1991). This is effectively a multi-sectoral, small, open, regional variant of the Layard, Nickell and Jackman (1991) model of imperfect competition in which all agents have perfect foresight and investment and consumption decisions are determined through a process of inter-temporal optimisation. The small, open-region assumption allows us to treat all external prices and the RUK economy as exogenous.[7]

Given the outcome of the referendum, we know that for the immediate future policy changes will be conducted under a continuing UK monetary union. Accordingly, we assume a permanently fixed exchange rate throughout our analysis. For simplicity we also assume a continuing fully integrated financial market. AMOS is a flexible modelling framework, which has been widely used for policy analysis. In this chapter we adopt the variant of the model presented in Lecca, McGregor and Swales (2012a) and Lecca et al. (2014), where model details can be found.[8]

Balanced budget Changes in income tax

According to the 2009 HM Treasury Budget estimate, the amount of additional revenue that the Scottish tax office would have been able to collect for a three pence rise in the Scottish income tax rate would be approximately £1.05 billion. This corresponds to a rise in the average income tax rate of 10.03 per cent. Accordingly, we simulate a 10.03 per cent rise in the Scottish income tax rate with the revenues being recycled to increase government consumption. We consider three scenarios, which differ in the assumptions made about the use and impact of the recycled revenues. In the first simulation, government expenditure is simply treated as current expenditure, which is assumed to have no direct beneficial supply-side effects. Examples might be spending on parks or library services. This is the conventional type of balanced budget fiscal expansion. However, where workers bargain over take-home pay, the rise in income tax has adverse supply-side effects as workers seek to restore their after-tax wage by pushing up wage claims and reducing competitiveness.

In the second case, public expenditure again does not generate a direct beneficial supply-side effect, but the potential negative supply-side impact is neutralised by the actions of potential migrants and through wage bargaining behaviour. In this case we assume that government expenditure is valued by residents and migrants. Public spending creates an amenity, whose value is reflected in migrants' decisions to move and in unions' bargaining behaviour. The idea here is similar to the notion of a 'social wage', in which unions moderate their wage claims in response to a hike in taxes provided these generate improved public services that their members genuinely value. (See Chapter 1 and Lecca et al. 2014.)

While in the first and second scenarios tax revenues fund government current expenditure, in the third scenario we assume that they fund government capital spending. In this case, the increase in government expenditure financed by the increase in income tax has explicit beneficial supply-side effects. This reflects the fact that in this case the additional revenue is recycled into public investment in infrastructure that increases the stock of public capital and, in turn, increases productivity in all sectors.

The focus of this chapter is primarily on the long run over which migration flows, driven by real wage and unemployment differentials between Scotland and RUK, and capital stock adjustments, driven by expected profitability, are complete. Accordingly, we begin by reporting the new steady-state equilibrium obtained as a result of a balanced budget fiscal expansion. These results are reported as percentage changes from base year values in Table 2.1.[9] We subsequently briefly consider the adjustment process to the new long-run equilibrium.

In the first and second columns of Table 2.1 we focus on the case of an income tax-funded expansion in public current consumption that has no direct supply-side effects. The first column of Table 2.1 reports the results for the current default version of our model of the Scottish economy. In this case a balanced budget expansion of government expenditure financed by income taxation has a negative impact on GDP and employment, which fall by 1.71 per cent and 1.65 per cent from their base year values respectively. There is a beneficial impact on aggregate demand because the stimulus to public expenditure is greater than the contractionary impact of lower (more import-intensive) consumption expenditure. Government expenditure increases by 2.98 per cent while household consumption falls by 1.15 per cent. However, the positive net effect on demand is more than offset by the adverse competitiveness effects of the rise in income taxation as labour pushes up wages to restore

Table 2.1 The long-run percentage changes in key Scottish economic variables as a result of a 4.9 per cent average increase in the Scottish income tax rate

	Scottish variable rate		
	Default	Social wage	Public capital
Change in income tax rate	10.03	10.03	10.03
GDP	−1.71	0.49	2.80
Consumer price index	1.11	0.00	−2.64
Unemployment rate	0.00	0.00	0.00
Total employment	−1.65	0.77	0.14
Nominal wage	3.68	0.00	−0.16
Nominal wage after tax	1.11	−2.48	−2.64
Real gross wage	2.55	0.00	2.55
Real wage after tax	0.00	−2.48	0.00
User cost of capital	1.04	0.00	−2.53
Population	−1.65	0.77	0.14
Household consumption	−1.15	−1.01	0.36
Government consumption	2.98	4.07	−
Investment by origin	−1.94	0.02	3.92
Public investment	−	−	68.68
RUK export	−1.69	0.00	5.24
ROW export	−1.63	0.00	4.78

their real take-home wage. Nominal and real wages rise by 3.68 per cent and 2.55 per cent respectively. The rise in the real wage generates an increase in the price of commodities reflected here in the *cpi* which in turn reduces exports to the RUK and the rest of the world (ROW). The initial decline in real wages and rise in the unemployment rate drive out-migration until equilibrium is restored with lower population but real post-tax wage and unemployment rates returning to their initial values.

In fact, the negative impact of a balanced budget fiscal expansion is not inevitable. In theory, the impact could go either way, since it reflects the net outcome of two countervailing forces: the stimulus to aggregate demand on the one hand and the adverse competitiveness effects on the other (Lecca et al. 2014). As far as the Scottish results are concerned, the adverse competitiveness effects predominate, an outcome that reflects the highly open nature of the Scottish economy, and its consequential sensitivity to competitiveness changes.

However, it transpires that the public's attitudes towards public expenditure and taxation are very important, to the extent that they can alter the sign of the balanced budget multiplier (Lecca et al. 2014). In particular, if unions in effect bargain over a 'social wage', in which the increase in public services arising from a balanced budget fiscal expansion are valued as much as the reduction in private consumption expenditures, the impact on the economy becomes positive. A key feature of the Nordic model, at least in its early form, was the tripartite system that characterised wage bargaining. Government, employers and strong, centralised unions bargained over wages (Keating and Harvey 2014). Such a mechanism is reflected in the results reported in the second column of Table 2.1. In this case, since the social wage is unchanged, the adverse competitiveness effects associated with bargaining over real take-home pay are eliminated, so that there is no upward pressure on the nominal wage. In this case we obtain a conventional Keynesian balanced budget multiplier result (albeit for the case with variable population and capital stocks), in which output and employment expand and there is no change in the nominal wage or prices. In fact, we observe an increase in GDP (0.49 per cent) and employment (0.77 per cent) and the negative competitiveness effects are completely eliminated, so that there are no changes in nominal wages, relative prices or exports. It should be noted, however, that the current Scottish wage bargaining system is significantly less centralised than might be required to produce this outcome. Ensuring a social wage outcome in these circumstances is particularly challenging; it is likely that significant institutional change would be required to emulate such a system.

UK-wide national bargaining currently remains important in Scotland, certainly for some sectors. This effectively creates an element of nominal wage inflexibility here as the UK wage is bargained at the UK level, and so is broadly fixed from a Scottish perspective. This, or indeed any other source of Scottish nominal wage inflexibility (such as prolonged-recession-induced weaker union bargaining power), also makes it more likely that a fiscal expansion would have positive effects since this inhibits (and in the limit prevents) the adverse competitiveness effects of the tax rise. However, it seems likely that UK-wide bargaining mechanisms would increasingly come under strain if a Scottish Government does indeed choose to pursue a distinctive income tax policy from that in RUK.

Moreover, the welfare effects of changes in spending level will depend on the public's evaluation of public services against private spending. There is some evidence from the USA, for example, that net in-migration responds positively to education and health spending, but is negatively related to welfare spending.[10] The final chapter of this book explores attitudes in the UK and in Scotland, suggesting that Scottish attitudes are not particularly favourable to more public expenditure when it is matched to tax rises. On the other hand, there is some evidence of willingness to pay more for specific services where the link can be made, a finding consistent with international experience (see Chapter 7).

The social investment model (Chapter 1), further, suggests that it is not simply public spending per se that matters, but also its composition. We turn next to a consideration of further aspect of the composition of government spending that seems to matter. According to Government Expenditure and Revenue Scotland (GERS) figures (2008 and 2013), for the year 2008–9 11 per cent of the budget was allocated to public capital expenditure while the rest is made up of current purchases of goods and services. This share falls to 9 per cent of the total budget for the period 2012–13. Here we explore the impact of a rise in this share through an income-tax-financed increase in infrastructure spending.

Recall that our default model assumes that the increase in government expenditure has no direct supply-side effects.

However, it transpires that if public expenditure does have beneficial supply-side effects then the prospects of a positive economic impact from a balanced budget fiscal expansion are again enhanced. The most obvious source of a beneficial supply-side impact is public capital expenditure, for example on infrastructure, which impacts directly on the economy's productive capacity. This acts at least to moderate and possibly even offset any adverse competitiveness effect and so potentially avoids the crowding out effects on private resources (Lecca, McGregor and Swales 2014). This is the outcome that we observe in the third column of Table 2.1.

The additional tax revenue increases public investment and, in turn, the stock of public capital available in the economy. Examples would be improvements in infrastructure, such as roads and telecommunications, which improve the productive efficiency of the economy as a whole. The services of the public capital stock are treated as an unpaid factor whose services are enjoyed to the same degree by all production sectors. The results suggest that the negative competitiveness effects of a rise in income tax rate are more than fully offset by the positive supply-side impacts of an increase in the public capital stock and the corresponding stimulus to productivity. There is in this case a significant increase in GDP, by 2.8 per cent from its base year value. Employment and consumption increase by 0.14 per cent and 0.36 per cent respectively. The supply-side stimulus coming from an increase in the stock of public capital is of a sufficient scale in this case that competitiveness actually improves overall, despite bargaining and migration being focused on the post-tax real wage. The fall in the nominal wage has beneficial effects on competitiveness, and there is an increase in exports to RUK and ROW in this case by 5.24 per cent and 4.78 per cent respectively. However, this result is not inevitable, since again the end result is the net effect of countervailing forces. In particular the net outcome depends crucially on the productivity of the infrastructure. If this is modest in scale the negative competitiveness effects would again predominate (Lecca, McGregor and Swales 2014).

While public capital expenditure is the most obvious example of public expenditure that we would expect to have a beneficial impact on the supply side of the economy, it is by no means the only one. As advocates of the social investment model have noted, many elements of what is currently classified as 'current' government expenditure are, in effect, investments in human capital. Spending on education is one example, where we would expect productivity to be stimulated directly as a consequence of public spending, potentially with significant economy-wide impacts. Hermannsson et al. (2014) analyse the impact of increased graduates in the labour market but elements of health and other public spending may be similarly regarded.

The dynamics of adjustment to the long-run equilibria discussed above are summarised in Figures 2.1 and 2.2. Figure 2.1 shows the adjustment path of GDP. In our default, conventional model GDP falls immediately and gradually adjusts to its long-run level. In contrast, in the social wage case GDP increases immediately and reaches the new long-run level quickly; in this case relative prices do not change and so adjustment is very rapid. When the tax rise is used to fund capital expenditure GDP falls for a very considerable period with the adverse supply effects dominating in the short run, but ultimately rises very significantly. Policy makers with a short time horizon could easily misjudge the policy impact in this case, or assess its benefits with an excessively high discount rate.

Figure 2.2 shows what is happening to the take-home real wage in each of these cases. In the default case the real wage falls initially in response to the tax hike, but gradually returns to

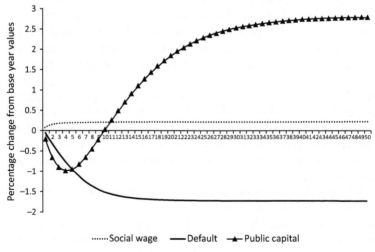

······Social wage   ——Default   —▲—Public capital

Figure 2.1 GDP impacts of balanced budget fiscal expansions.

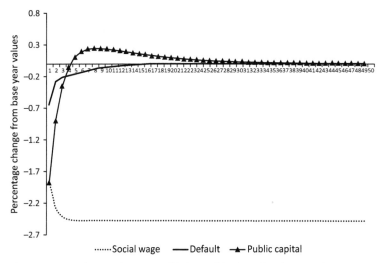

Figure 2.2 Real wage impacts of balanced budget fiscal expansions.

its initial level. In the 'social wage' case the social wage is maintained, but because of the increase in government expenditures which are valued, this allows a permanent reduction in the real take-home wage. When spending is on infrastructure, the real take-home wage falls significantly initially, but recovers rapidly and indeed overshoots its long-run equilibrium level before converging on that (with zero percentage change).

Scottish-specific changes in the rate of corporation tax

While corporation tax is not presently devolved this continues to be strongly supported by some groups, notably the SNP Government, and so we consider the possible effects of this, under an assumption that any change in rates is negotiated with the UK Government along the lines that have been agreed for devolution to Northern Ireland.[11]

The change in corporation tax we consider is the earlier proposal by the Scottish Government, to implement a balanced budget reduction in corporation tax rates from 23 per cent to 20 per cent.[12] We abstract from the possible complication of transfer pricing and headquarter movement that could add to the positive, or mitigate any negative, effects of the tax. The results of our model suggest that a reduction in corporation tax financed by a corresponding increase in the rate of income tax generates negative[13] effects on the economy in the long run, as inspection of the first column of results in Table 2.2 confirms. GDP, employment and consumption all fall below their base year values. The positive effects generated by a reduction in the corporation tax rate are reflected in an increase in private investment of 0.17 per cent from its base year value. A reduction in corporation tax lowers the cost of capital, which stimulates investment demand, as capital is substituted for labour in production. However, in this case the positive change in investment is more than offset by the adverse effects of an increase in the average rate of income tax of 2.33 per cent, which reduces private consumption by 0.47 per cent. Furthermore, the rise in income tax puts upward pressure on wages, as workers seek to restore their real consumption wage, increasing the prices of commodities and offsetting the potential beneficial

Table 2.2 Long-run impacts of a three percentage point reduction in corporation tax changes (with offsetting adjustments in income tax or government expenditure)

	Corporation tax	
	Offset: income tax	Offset: Government expediture
Income tax rate	2.33	0.00
GDP	−0.33	0.56
Consumer price index	0.17	−0.36
Unemployment rate	0.00	0.00
Total employment	−0.62	0.25
Nominal wage	1.36	−0.36
Nominal wage after tax	0.17	−0.36
Real gross wage	1.19	0.00
Real wage after tax	0.00	0.00
User cost of capital	0.13	−0.37
Population	−0.62	0.25
Household consumption	−0.47	0.13
Government consumption	–	−1.22
Private investment	0.17	1.16
Public investment	–	–
RUK export	−0.06	0.76
ROW export	−0.17	0.62

competitiveness effects of a lower cost of capital. Accordingly, RUK and ROW exports fall by 0.06 per cent and 0.17 per cent respectively.

However, a rather different long-run impact occurs when, instead of increasing income tax, government reduces its expenditure. In these circumstances the positive effects obtained by a reduced capital cost are such as to overwhelm the negative impact on aggregate demand caused by a fall of 1.22 per cent in government consumption. Accordingly, investment expenditure increases by 1.16 per cent which, together with the improvement in competitiveness due to a reduction in commodity prices that stimulates exports, produces an increase in GDP, employment and consumption of 0.56 per cent, 0.25 per cent and 0.13 per cent respectively.

Notice that in the second simulation the social wage will actually be falling, since government expenditure is falling. If we were to allow for restoration of the social wage through a hike in nominal wages, the adverse competitiveness effects would predominate.

In this simulation we have not allowed for any additional stimulus that might arise through greater inward investment (Foreign Direct Investment or FDI). Government expenditure could actually increase if a stimulus to FDI is allowed for, so that there is a possibility of the change ultimately becoming 'self-funding' as the SNP has claimed. This outcome was used in evidence by the Scottish Government (2011a) and its source is Lecca, McGregor and Swales (2012b). Of course, such a beneficial outcome would be reinforced if in this case bargaining included the social wage, because government expenditure would rise.

Recall that this analysis assumes no retaliation from trading partners including other parts of the UK, since the assumption is a negotiated reduction in the corporation tax rate. Retaliation would undoubtedly reduce the benefits of the change.[14] On the other hand, no technology spillover effects from FDI were included, nor were possible endogenous growth effects, both of which would reinforce the positive effects of the corporation tax cut.

The adjustment paths for GDP for both corporation tax simulations are presented in Figure 2.3. In both cases GDP falls initially, but more so in the income tax recycling case. In the case where government expenditure is cut, adjustment quickly

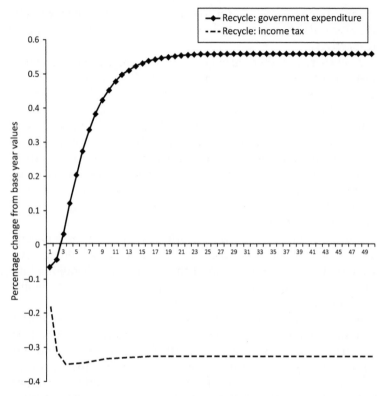

Figure 2.3 GDP impacts of balanced budget corporation tax cut.

becomes positive and GDP rises to its new long-run equilibrium. Where income taxes are raised to finance the reduction in corporation tax, GDP falls significantly, and does not recover.

Throughout our analysis we have so far assumed that individuals and groups behave in a rational economic manner. This implies, among other things, that individuals do not suffer from money illusion. So, for example, workers bargain over their *real* wages. There is some evidence from the behavioural economics literature that this assumption may be inappropriate. For example, workers might be more likely to notice, and react to, changes in income tax rates, but less likely to react to a failure to adjust allowances to counter fiscal drag. This suggests that the SNP's tax plans (not raising the threshold for the higher tax rate as much as in the rest of the UK) are less likely to stimulate wage claims than are the rises in income tax rates proposed by the Labour, Liberal Democrat and Green parties at the 2016 Scottish election. Furthermore, the greater the degree of nominal wage inflexibility (which can result from UK-wide wage bargaining), the more likely it is that any balanced budget expansion would in practice prove to have an expansionary impact on the economy.

Other aspects of the Scotland Act (2016): fiscal responsibility and the link between economic growth and tax revenues; social union, 'fairness' and well-being

Two related features of the referendum debate continue to characterise aspects of the conversation over further devolution of fiscal powers. These are: fiscal responsibility and the link between economic growth and tax revenues, which the SNP Government claim as a major advantage of independence; and the notion that Scots prefer a more equitable and fairer society than that legislated for by Westminster governments. Of course, independence per se is not a necessary condition to allow the Scottish Government greater influence in these areas. A greater degree of fiscal autonomy ensures a closer link between economic growth and tax revenues, while also allowing enhanced impact on equity and well-being in Scotland. It is interesting to consider what powers would be required to allow the Scottish Government to have a significant influence over these issues, since this seems likely to impact on public attitudes to the most recent Scotland Act. We seek to inform our discussion of these topics by drawing on the lessons of the simulations we have discussed above, as well as other relevant considerations.

Under the previous fiscal arrangements, where the Barnett formula governed the block grant distribution to the devolved administrations, the fiscal benefits from any increase in the growth of the Scottish economy went to Westminster, irrespective of the source of growth. Equally, however, the impact of slower growth in the Scottish economy was mitigated by the fact that its ability to spend does not decline automatically as its contribution to UK tax revenues declines. Indeed some key elements of welfare benefits – funded by Westminster – operate counter-cyclically. The argument is that this reduced the incentive for voters to vote for, and the devolved Scottish Government to implement, strategies for increased economic growth.[15] Furthermore, that system limited the fiscal responsibility of the Scottish Government since it was unable – and was not required – to raise the revenue to fund its own expenditures.

As we have seen, income taxation is substantially devolved under the Scotland Act (2016). The adjustment to the block grant to reflect the anticipated actual revenue from the subset of taxes that are devolved will enhance incentives to grow the economy but equally increase exposure to revenue risk.[16] This mechanism is embodied within our analysis of balanced budget tax changes above. The Scottish Government feels the full effects of the consequences of any income tax changes that it makes. If income tax revenues decline as a consequence of its decisions, then so too must its expenditures (and vice versa).

Other devolved taxes, such as the Land and Building Transactions Tax, which replaces Stamp Duty, also add to the link between tax revenues and economic activity in Scotland, but these are very modest in scale.

Overall, the stronger the link between tax revenues and Scottish economic activity, the greater will be the incentive to adopt growth-stimulating policies. However, there is a risk that revenues may fluctuate and be insufficient to allow desired spending. There is little doubt that this benefit – and associated risk – of greater tax devolution will remain a key feature of the continuing debate on greater fiscal autonomy. While the SNP Government chose to emphasise the potential positive dimension, particularly in respect of corporation tax changes and child support provision (see below), there is, of course, a potential downside to the revenue-activity link.[17]

Tax rates need not be devolved in their entirety to establish a link between tax revenues raised in Scotland and economic activity here. The Scotland Act (2016) will result in the assignment of 50 per cent of Scottish VAT revenues to the Scottish Government from 2019–20. This assignment increases the overall sensitivity of Scottish Government revenues to economic activity, but simultaneously increases revenue risk. Would revenues to the Scottish Government be stable enough to maintain stability in the provision of public services? We shall explore this in future research. We now discuss aspects of the interregional linkages of tax bases created by the block grant adjustment.

We focus almost exclusively on the likely impact of the Scotland Act on Scotland and the Scottish economy. However,

Scotland and the RUK economies are inextricably interlinked, with common financial and labour markets as well as extensive trade flows. While our analysis so far recognises the openness of the Scottish economy, especially with respect to the RUK economy, but also to ROW, we have not explicitly considered the impact of interdependence.

The proposed block grant adjustment method, (IPC), makes Scottish public finances continue to be dependent upon the economy, and tax base, of the UK as a whole, of which Scotland represents less than 10 per cent on any measure of aggregate economic activity. Interregional interdependence of the Scottish public finances is explicitly built into the new arrangements, and the growth in the Scottish *relative to* the RUK tax base is a crucial issue in the block grant adjustment. Nonetheless, the weight of the block grant in governing Scottish public finances will be weakened, as therefore will the dependence on the UK economy as a whole.

Amior, Crawford and Tetlow's (2013) projections provide a basis for an initial consideration of the longer-term pressures on Scotland's public finances, although their focus was on the fiscal position of an independent Scotland. Amior, Crawford and Tetlow (2013) identify two negative long-term pressures on Scotland's public finances relative to RUK. The first is that Scotland's population is projected to age more rapidly than that of RUK, and so pressures on expenditure increase while the working population declines. Of course, the pressures on expenditures would have been present under the previous fiscal arrangements, given that the Barnett formula was unrelated to needs, and they remain a challenge under the new arrangements. However, if, as seems likely, the presence of more rapid ageing in Scotland leads to a shrinking workforce and lower tax revenues, the fiscal pressures would be even greater under the current regime, as spending is now (partially) tied to such revenues.

Second, Amior, Crawford and Tetlow (2013) argued that North Sea Oil revenues are likely to decline through time as reserves become exhausted. Already, the collapse of oil prices has resulted in a major adverse impact on the Scottish economy and on the Scottish Government's public finances (GERS 2016). Since Scotland remains part of the UK, the immediate impact on Scottish public finances is substantially mitigated. However, oil has an asymmetric impact on Scotland and RUK, so that the pressures on public finances under the new fiscal arrangements are greater than under those it replaces, since the fall in tax revenues arising from an oil-induced contraction in economic activity will now impact on government spending, even though the taxation of oil itself is not devolved. Of course, the challenges would be substantially greater under independence, since Scotland's expenditure would depend partly on oil revenues.

While the continuation of the union provides some insulation against these developments, the prospect of greater tax devolution ensures that differential Scotland and RUK developments in population and economic activity would reduce the Scottish block grant at the margin, as the Scottish tax base would fall relative to the RUK's, although the per capita nature of the agreed adjustment would protect Scotland from differential population growth over the first five years.[18, 19] However, while Barnett, which is population-based, has acted so as to maintain differential public expenditure per head, we strongly suspect that the current allocation significantly exceeds needs. Accordingly, while Barnett precludes the kind of response to an ageing population that a needs-based system would generate, Scotland's preferential current position provides a significant buffer.

While instructive, the mechanistic nature of Amior, Crawford and Tetlow's projections should be kept in mind. In particular, these projections do not allow for possible Scottish Government action to use economic growth to improve the deficit and debt-to-GDP ratios. Governments do have the *potential*, at least, to 'grow their way out of trouble'. They will be unable to address the issue through adoption of distinctive immigration policies, except perhaps at the margin by a revival of the former Fresh Talent Initiative. So the key issue is whether a Scottish Government post implementation of the Scotland Acts (2012, 2016) can in fact grow the Scottish economy more rapidly than before.

The degree of integration of the Scottish and RUK economies implies that there are likely to be significant interregional spillover and feedback effects (Gilmartin et al. 2013). This was recognised by the Smith Commission through its 'no detriment' principle. The Fiscal Framework adopted in 2016 to allocate the remaining block grant defines this narrowly so that only direct effects on the public budgets need to be taken into account routinely. Yet system-wide spillover effects may be substantial

(Lecca, McGregor and Swales 2015). In these circumstances UK welfare as a whole could be enhanced by coordination of policies between Scottish and Westminster Governments, when significant powers are devolved. The problems of institutional design to achieve this are addressed in Chapter 6.

Fairness, well-being and the nature of Scottish society

A key feature of the referendum debate was discussion of whether Scots really desired a more equitable and fairer society. Given the subsequent decision to stay in the union but enhance devolution, the question is whether the new devolution settlement can provide policies that significantly influence equity or fairness?

The Conservative, Labour and Liberal Democrat parties all, in effect, emphasise the importance of 'social union' in the UK, maintaining the potential for comparable quality public services and core welfare payments, such as unemployment benefits and pensions across the UK, although the argument was put most explicitly by Labour. Indeed, maintenance of the union was Labour's rationale for its more limited proposals on the devolution of income taxes and welfare benefits. However, not all were convinced – including Conservatives and Social Democrats – that acceptance of the argument for a continuing social union implied quite the limitations on devolved powers that Labour initially judged to be appropriate, and that view predominated in the Smith Commission and ultimately the Scotland Act (2016).

Of course, the scale of the tax and expenditure changes required to emulate the Nordic model would be considerably in excess of those we simulated in the preceding section of the chapter. Clearly, the bigger the tax and expenditure changes the greater would be the pressure on take-home pay, and this could increase the difficulty of persuading the Scottish electorate to value the corresponding change in the social wage sufficiently. So, for example, raising the average tax rate by five pence, ten pence and fifteen pence would, in our simulations, generate a roughly 4 per cent, 8 per cent and 12 per cent reduction in real take-home wages.

A Scottish Government could conceivably argue that changing income tax bands, and having higher rates bite at lower nominal income levels, could be justified given that there are far fewer very high income earners than in the UK as a whole, and the lower of living in Scotland. However, none of the parties has adopted such a position, and nor are there regional consumer price indices available that would allow a systematic comparison of relative living standards. A Scottish consumer price index could, however, be produced.

However, one of the key mechanisms for tacking inequality is the extent of *progressivity* of the tax system in general and the income tax system in particular. Both the Labour Party and the Green Party propose making the income tax system more progressive. While our own analysis relates to the adjustment of an 'average tax rate', we can use our results to inform a discussion of introducing more progressivity. We know that higher-income individuals bear a disproportionate share of total income tax (Bell 2013). On the other hand, higher-income individuals tend to be more mobile, and the worry is that differential progressivity in the Scottish and RUK tax systems may lead to net out-migration of these individuals and a reduced tax base. Against this, social wage and public investment arguments can again provide a countervailing force, but the marginal cost of adopting a social wage approach in the face of greater progressivity of the tax system would be significantly higher for members of high-income groups, and so the net effect would likely be higher net out-migration (lower in-migration) of those in this income group.

Conclusion

Scotland currently has high levels of government expenditure per head and significant devolved powers over the distribution of public spending. The Barnett formula, whose application in practice has had the effect of maintaining a beneficial settlement for Scotland in public spending shares, will continue to apply even after the implementation of the Fiscal Framework (2016) and the Scotland Act (2016), albeit subject to a block grant adjustment to reflect the extent of devolved taxes and assigned revenues and the transfer of responsibility for welfare. This greater fiscal responsibility of increased devolution of tax powers will strengthen the link between Scottish economic activity and the Scottish Government's budget, and lead to an enhancement of the Scottish Parliament's ability to deal with financial matters. This increases the incentive to the Scottish Government and electorate to promote growth-stimulating policies, but also increases the downside risk of fluctuations in tax revenues and public spending. The Scotland Acts (2012, 2016) will certainly allow the Scottish Parliament considerable choice over the general *levels* of taxation and government spending. The Government will be able to choose to move the economy to higher taxes and higher spend in the direction of the Scandinavian social investment model or, less likely, to the low tax/low spend Baltic model. Our analysis suggests that the structure of the Scottish economy provides something of a challenge in that the degree of openness of the Scottish economy makes it particularly sensitive to any changes in competitiveness induced by rises in taxation. However, such effects can be countered if the public spending has significant supply-side impacts through infrastructure investment, although these impacts typically take a long time to build up and therefore may not be valued appropriately by a government that has a comparatively short lifespan.

The adverse competitiveness effects of higher taxation can also be countered if the Scottish public can be persuaded of the importance of its *social* wage (not just take-home pay) and the Scottish Government correctly identifies the types of public expenditures that are regarded as important to the social wage, most likely health and education spending. However, what evidence there is suggests that welfare spending may be unlikely to figure largely, if at all, in the social wage, which could prove problematic if a Scottish Government were to engage in a balanced budget fiscal expansion to fund such expenditure. Of course, while public attitudes to taxes and public spending matter, these are not immutable, and may be amenable to change in response to effective political leadership; it may be that there is the potential for widespread support for universal benefits such as pensions.

The greater devolution of income taxation therefore does provide an opportunity to make real choices over the type of society that the Scottish people want, and a higher tax and spend economy is likely to be a more equal one although the extent to which greater equality is achieved is dependent upon the precise composition of both tax revenues and expenditures. The Scotland Act (2016) does provide for considerable control over the degree of *progressivity* of income taxation, a major potential mechanism through which inequality may be tackled, in principle. Indeed the Labour Party and the Greens have proposed making the system more progressive, with significant rises in the highest rate of income tax (of five and fifteen percentage points respectively).

However, the concerns that surround the likely consequences of a hike in average income tax rates apply with even greater force to varying the degree of progressivity of the income tax system, given the dependence of the overall income tax base on high-income earners who enjoy higher geographic mobility. Of course, the same mitigating factors apply, but with less force given, for example, the higher marginal cost to this group of maintaining or enhancing the social – at the expense of the private – wage. Naturally, the problem would be accentuated by an attempt to move very substantially in the direction of the Scandinavian economies since substantial cuts in real take-home pay would be required under the social wage model. In this sense, at least, there may be a real trade-off between the desire to incentivise growth and the expressed desire for a more equal society.

Equality and well-being also depend on the distribution of spending as well as taxation. Education and health typically feature in indicators of aggregate well-being, and these are already under the control of the Scottish Government (although aggregate spending capacity will continue, in part, to reflect the block grant), but the greatest beneficiaries of such expenditures are not necessarily the poorest. Elements of the welfare system are devolved, but central parts of it continue to be reserved.

A number of extensions of our analysis would be useful. First, we intend to extend our more formal analysis to accommodate the details of the Fiscal Framework (2016). An attempt to provide a comprehensive analysis of the potential economic impact of using the new fiscal powers, including the degree of progressivity of the income tax system, would be helpful to inform coherent policy development and evaluation. Second, we have so far mainly considered the operation of taxes in isolation – albeit with balanced budget adjustments in expenditures of different kinds – and it would be useful to explore the likely consequences of alternative packages/combinations of policy changes, with a view to maximising the beneficial impacts on the economy.

Third, we have focused here on the use of balanced budget changes in *non-welfare* expenditures. There is perhaps a perception that a fairer society may require higher expenditures on welfare, and in subsequent work it would be interesting to explore the impact of tax-financed welfare changes, although it seems likely that the social wage concept may be less compelling for such changes. Fourth, we have recently extended our model to incorporate household disaggregation (by income group/household type), so that we can now identify any impacts of policy changes on the distribution of income. Fifth, it would be instructive to explore the consequences of the Scottish Government using its enhanced borrowing powers, for example, to finance increased infrastructure spending.

Sixth, in this chapter we have focused almost exclusively on the likely effects of further devolution on the Scottish economy. Our analysis is impacted significantly by the extent of integration of the Scottish and RUK economies, but we have made no attempt here to model the *interdependence* of these economies. This will prove crucial to a full analysis of Scottish, and indeed Westminster, policies. The interdependence is apparent simply from inspection of the extent of integration of goods markets, reflected in the scale of interregional trade flows, and in common labour and financial markets. The Scottish public budget is likely to continue to depend importantly on the time path of the RUK tax base, as well as Scotland's, and there are long-term pressures towards divergence that are challenging for Scotland, although the block grant adjustment mechanism ensures that, at least for the next five years, Scotland's public expenditure is insulated against Scotland's population growth rate being lower than that of the UK. The Fiscal Framework (2016) proposes recognising the no detriment principle advocated by the Smith Commission, but in a fairly narrow sense of direct spillovers to public sector budgets. Indirect spillovers will not typically be recognised, but these may well prove to be substantial (Lecca, McGregor and Swales 2015). A full interregional analysis of policy, including the prospects for coordination of policy between the central and devolved Governments is a matter of some urgency given the timescale for implementation of the Fiscal Framework.

Finally, the new focus on UK-wide constitutional issues resulting from the referendum debate and its aftermath suggests the desirability of extending our analysis to the other nations and regions of the UK and perhaps to sub-regions of England. The immediate challenge that this extension raises is the availability of appropriate quality data. While the Scottish Government has led on the provision of own-region data, others have achieved less, no doubt in part because of resource limitations. If we are to live in a quasi-federal UK with a regionally differentiated tax system, we need to consider the appropriate provision of data to facilitate informed decision making, such as regional-specific consumer price indices that allow interregional comparisons of real living standards, and reliable data on interregional trade flows that would facilitate accurate tracking of the interdependence of UK regional economies. In this context the initial focus on the Scottish case will still prove valuable as it, in effect, provides a laboratory in which innovative policies can be explored and, depending on the outcome, can be emulated or avoided by other devolved authorities.

Acknowledgement

*   The authors are grateful to David Bell, Alastair Greig, Kevin Kane, Michael Keating, Scherie Nicol, Jeremy Peat and Graeme Roy for comments on an earlier draft and to Stewart Dunlop for research assistance.

Notes

1. O'Donnell (2013) sets out some guiding principles for fiscal policy and constitutional change.
2. The Scottish Government introduced the rates and bands for the LBTT in its draft budget statement on 9 October 2014. This will also have regional impacts within Scotland, and there are other considerations that transactions taxes raise more generally. See for example Gibb (2013).
3. Other methods of BGA were considered including own base deduction, in which the block grant effectively offsets the impact of any Scottish tax change. See Holtham (2010) and Bell (2013) for a fuller discussion.
4. In fact, the analysis of changes in NI contributions would closely follow that of income tax changes (see below). There has been some discussion of devolving employers' NI contributions and Northern Ireland has a separate NI Fund.
5. The SNP also committed to increasing childcare, but argued this would be self-funding.

6. This is not to deny that some proposals could have significant effects, e.g. the SNP's commitment to increase carers' allowance, abolish the bedroom tax and establish a separate Scottish Social Security Agency.

7. For an explicitly interregional extension see Gilmartin et al. (2013) and Lecca, McGregor and Swales (2015).

8. The model is calibrated using a Scottish-specific Social Accounting Matrix (SAM) for the year 2009. This is based on the latest available input-output table for Scotland at the time this model was developed. Input-output tables are published with a substantial lag. However, economic structure does not change rapidly, so this is unlikely to have a substantial impact on our results.

9. The results are dependent to a degree on the values of certain key parameters of the model and on the precise treatment of migration flows. This is discussed, and sensitivity analyses are reported, in Lecca et al. (2014) and Lecca, McGregor and Swales (2014).

10. There is also some evidence, however, that short-distance moves for low-income households are positively linked to welfare benefits.

11. The expectation is that the Northern Ireland rate of corporation tax will be reduced to 12.5 per cent – the same rate as that in the Republic of Ireland – from April 2018. The UK Government consider this to be a special case, reflecting the shared border with the Republic of Ireland.

12. The Scottish Government's (2013) independence White Paper proposed to cut corporation tax to three points below the UK level.

13. The SNP did not say that it would increase income tax but this is a necessary corollary since, even if cutting corporation tax increased the tax base in the long term, the budget would still have to be balanced in the short term.

14. Darby, Ferret and Wooton (2014) provide an analysis which suggests that a small peripheral region like Scotland might gain from reducing corporation tax even when there is retaliation, since the latter will be only partial given that other regions retain their advantages of size and centrality.

15. Note that while incentives for voters and the government change, those for workers and firms do not.

16. See Holtham (2010). Increased devolution of taxes necessarily increases revenue risk.

17. The 'growth incentive' argument implies that a devolved Scottish Government (with no control over taxation) should have been less concerned about economic growth than its UK counterpart. This is an idea for which there appears to be little supporting evidence.

18. Furthermore, IPC may not be the chosen method of adjusting the block grant for all taxes.
19. However, the operation of the Barnett formula, given that Scotland's favourable base year share of public spending was high, implies Scotland benefited from lower population.

3 Inequality in Scotland: Dimensions and Policy Responses

David Bell, David Eiser and Katerina Lisenkova

Introduction

Inequality has become a touchstone issue in political debate across the developed world. Stagnant or declining living standards among the low paid have given the lie to belief in the 'trickle down' effect where unfettered markets would generate benefits for the poor as well as the rich. The lack of such effects has been associated with growing disenchantment with the incumbent political class who seem impotent or unwilling to introduce policies that would increase the living standards of poor people, and in turn this disenchantment has been associated with the emergence of new political movements of the right and left.

Having been ignored for decades by international economic organisations, inequality is now viewed not only as an issue of social justice, but also as an impediment to economic growth by organisations including the OECD (Cingano 2014), the World Bank (2014), the IMF (Dabla-Norris et al. 2015) and the European Union (2015). Within Scottish politics, inequality played an important role in the constitutional debate. Successive Scottish governments have been committed to tackling inequalities, sometimes drawing on myths about the Scottish egalitarian tradition. This chapter explores inequality in Scotland and the scope for policy intervention by the Scottish Government to reduce its level or to mitigate its effects. To put these issues in perspective, the next section considers inequality within its wider national and international context, beginning with an initial examination of the concept of inequality. We go on to consider alternative theories of its drivers and the extent to which its growth may be susceptible to policy intervention at the Scottish level. We also highlight the importance of intergenerational inequality – the extent to which generations place burdens on, or transfer benefits to, future generations. This occupies an important position in the current inequality debate.

We then consider whether sub-state governments (SSGs) can successfully introduce their own form of interventions to reduce inequality and the extent to which these are constrained by national policy frameworks. If Scotland wished to pursue its own inequality strategy, its freedom to do so is inevitably constrained by UK economic policies and by the UK institutional and legal environment. The following section summarises what we know about inequality in Scotland, while the final section concludes with some discussion of the opportunities available to the Scottish Government to influence inequality in Scotland.

Inequality: concepts and drivers

Studies of economic inequality focus typically on differences in the income of the rich compared with the poor. Income is relatively easy to measure. Studies of inequalities in wealth, or in access to economic opportunities, are also common, but are less frequent than studies of income inequality, principally because it is more difficult to find reliable and accurate measures of wealth and opportunity. Income inequality is generally measured in relation to individuals or to households. However, inequalities between groups of individuals can also be revealing. In this chapter we group individuals of the same age and discuss inequalities between generations – intergenerational inequality. This form of inequality has been largely ignored in policy debates on inequality in Scotland.

Income inequality can be measured before and after the effects of taxes and benefits. The difference between these measures provides a way of measuring the effectiveness of tax and benefit policies in redistributing income from rich to poor (Bell and Eiser 2015b).

This chapter also explores the implications of policy instruments to address inequality being available to different levels of government and the possibility that these levels of government differ in their approaches to policy relating to inequality.

There are three main explanations of recent trends in income inequality. It is important to distinguish between these accounts of the drivers of inequality since their policy implications differ widely. The first explanation suggests that increasing inequality derives from factors largely outside the control of national governments. Chief among these are globalisation and skill-biased technological change. Globalisation exerts downward pressure on the earnings of the less qualified in developed countries working in the traded goods sector who find themselves competing with similar workers in less developed countries that are paid considerably less. The better qualified – those with higher levels of human capital –- do not face such stiff competition and experience less downward pressure on their wages. Technological change is described as 'skill biased' because it is a complement to skilled labour but a substitute for unskilled labour. Because the productivity of the skilled rises relative to the poor, so too do the wages of the skilled relative to the unskilled. The consequence is increased inequality. One specific form of technical change – computerisation – has reduced the demand for unskilled labour, increasing the wage gap between skilled and unskilled workers and hence increasing income inequality (Autor, Levy and Murnane 2003). Policy responses to this explanation of inequality generally emphasise the need to increase workers' skill levels.

The second explanation is based on the work of Piketty (2014), who suggests that income and wealth inequality have been growing since the eighteenth century. The economic disruption caused by the First and Second World Wars arrested that growth, but it has since returned to levels seen at the beginning of the twentieth century. Greater inequality is driven by the market system in which the returns to capital typically grow faster than the economy itself. Whereas in the past the owners of capital may have extracted substantial rents and so concentrated income and wealth among a relatively small group of individuals, Piketty argues that in more recent times the growth of large companies where senior executives are able to influence the size of their own rewards has led to a similar concentration of income and wealth. His policy recommendations are for a global tax on capital and perhaps for greater controls over executive pay. Progress on these policies is likely to be slow due to the difficulty of achieving international consensus on their design and implementation, and the fiscal advantages to those countries that opt out of the agreement.

The third explanation draws on the work of Joseph Stiglitz, a member of the Scottish Government's Council of Economic Advisers. He suggests that Piketty confuses capital with wealth (Stiglitz 2015). Aggregate wealth has been growing much more rapidly than the economy's effective capital stock. Much of the increase in wealth, he argues, is due to capital gains on assets and is concentrated among the owners of these assets. Market prices for these assets are pushed well above their economic productivity. For example, the value of the housing stock has increased substantially but without a commensurate increase in its productivity, even though it is part of the nation's capital stock. The appropriate policy response to asset price inflation is to reduce the opportunities for capital gains on assets.

He also argues that market failure has a role in explaining the increase in inequality. Monopoly rents emerge from the use of political influence to affect outcomes in, for example, the development of land, natural resources, technology and the financial sector. These 'exploitation' rents lead to higher profits, lower wages and higher firm valuations, without any real increase in the underlying wealth of the nation. The policy response is to reduce the opportunities for market manipulation.

To summarise, there are three main contenders for the explanation of recent rises in inequality. The first relates to technical change and globalisation to which the likely policy response would involve changing the industrial structure and the skills mix of the population. The second involves the divergence between wealth and national output and, given high levels of capital mobility, one possible, though extremely difficult, policy response is concerted international action to tax wealth. Finally, if increasing inequality is due to the divergences between wages and productivity, then there is some form of market failure within the labour market that might justify direct policy intervention to reduce opportunities for manipulating incomes by those with market power.

These arguments, which dominate the debate on income inequality, concentrate on inequality measured across the whole population at a single point in time. However, it is also valid to think of income inequality between age groups and how these evolve. For example, in the UK, the incomes of pensioner households have caught up with the incomes of non-pensioner households. Indeed, in 2015, after taking housing costs into account, pensioner incomes surpassed those of non-pensioner households for the first time, both in Scotland and in the UK as a whole (Belfield et al. 2015).

Explanations of changes in the wealth of the young relative to the old include rapidly rising asset prices (notably housing) during earlier decades, as well as generous pension arrangements. Since monetary and pension policy remain reserved to the UK, the Scottish Government has had little influence on these developments. Further, these trends have been accentuated by recent UK government policy on state benefits, which has tended to protect pensioner benefits in real terms while allowing working age benefits to fall in real terms. The welfare benefits that have been transferred to the Scottish Parliament are largely focused on the disabled and on older people, so there is limited scope for the Scottish Parliament to alter the balance between the income of pensioner and non-pensioner households.

Despite the changes in the relative fortunes of older and younger generations, it remains the case that intragenerational inequality is much higher than intergenerational inequality. But wealth is increasingly concentrated among the older generation. This has important implications from an inequality perspective. Assets that increase in value while they are held effectively impose an implicit tax on subsequent generations. Inheritance thus becomes increasingly important for younger generations, influencing the extent to which individuals can afford to purchase housing or access education. Since it is typically high-income earners that accumulate wealth, rising intergenerational inequality accentuates intragenerational inequality, which influences not only wealth holdings but also access to economic opportunities.

The discussion of intergenerational inequality thus far has simply compared two generations at a point in time. But clearly incomes evolve over the course of a lifetime. Perhaps we should not be concerned that the incomes of the young decline relative to those of the old, as long as the currently young eventually benefit to the same extent as they age. Indeed, a large part of the role of the welfare state is to redistribute not between individuals at a point in time, but across each individual's lifetime. Recent research (Levell, Roantree and Shaw 2015) finds that more than half of the redistribution achieved by taxes and benefits in the UK is over lifetimes rather than among different people. In this respect, the welfare state can be seen as a form of insurance pool, protecting against both temporary difficulties and the demands of the later stages of life.

Recognising the concept of lifetime income allows us to consider differences between generations in a slightly different light. More generous public spending on elderly benefits including pensions and healthcare will benefit those who are currently young, so long as those policies are maintained into the future. Indeed, there is a case for arguing that the currently young will benefit disproportionately from these policies, if increases in life expectancy continue to outstrip increases in the state pension age, and the state pension continues to be increased at a higher rate than inflation. But then the key question becomes whether the existing set of policies – including the fiscal promises made to current and future generations – is sustainable in the context of current and forecast tax revenues.

One of the methodologies which formally analyses these issues is generational accounting, originally developed by Auerbach, Gokhale and Kotlikoff (1991) and Kotlikoff (1992). Generational accounts (GAs) are designed to show the net discounted lifetime contribution that people in different cohorts are expected to make to the Exchequer. The resulting calculations show the degree to which the government is redistributing income between different generations – past, present and future – based on fiscal commitments made, demographic forecasts, and assumptions about productivity growth. McCarthy, Sefton and Weale's (2011) estimated GAs for the UK based on 2008 data suggest that those born in 2008 will make a net contribution to the Exchequer of £68,000; while future generations will each have to contribute almost £160,000 for the government to stay solvent in the long term. This suggests that current intergenerational transfers are unsustainable, and imply substantial tax increases, or reductions in public service provision, in future. This argument presents an interesting paradox. Policies for reducing inequality within the current population might involve increased public spending on, say, benefits. But this policy will increase the current deficit and impose a burden on future generations, thus conflicting with the objective of reducing intergenerational inequality. In contrast, tax increases reduce both inter-and intragenerational inequality. However, not only are tax increases unpopular with the electorate, they may result in negative responses from workers and consumers, thus undermining the economic growth on which the well-being of future generations depends.

Sub-state government policies to reduce inequality

Whereas national governments often introduce policies aimed at reducing inequality, the role and effectiveness of SSGs in relation to inequality is much less widely debated. SSGs may play a role in relation to any of the dimensions of inequality discussed in the previous section, but, as we shall see, this role is likely to be heavily constrained by national powers and institutions.

At the outset it is worth considering the range of policy levers through which government policy may influence inequality (Table 3.1). Almost all government policies have some distributional consequences and therefore affect levels of inequality (Atkinson 2015).

Some policies influence the distribution of income before the deduction of taxes and payment of benefits. Labour market policy can influence pre-tax income through, for example, the setting of minimum wages, wage bargaining arrangements and regulations controlling labour market contracts. France introduced a law in 2000 to limit the standard working week to 35 hours. By limiting the variation in weekly hours, and therefore in weekly income, this measure had the indirect effect of constraining pre-tax income inequality in France compared with the UK, where the Working Time Directive places a much

Table 3.1 Policy for addressing inequality

Fiscal policy	Wider government policy
Personal taxation	Labour-market policy
Property/land/wealth taxation	Product market regulation
Low-income/out-of-work benefits	(competition and innovation policy)
Sickness/disability benefits	Capital/financial market regulation
Old-age benefits	Overall macroeconomic stance
Public spending policy (e.g. education, health)	(e.g. inflation vs. employment targeting)
Public sector wage-setting policy	Moral suasion

higher limit of 48 hours per week on working time. The 35-hour working time limit has a dampening effect on the inequality of pre-tax incomes.

Fiscal policy, on the other hand, focuses on redistribution of market incomes through the personal tax and welfare system. The imposition of taxes and the payment of benefits tend to reduce the gap between the rich and poor. Thus, inequality of pre-tax incomes is always greater than that after the application of taxes and benefits.

But fiscal policy can also affect pre-tax income indirectly, by influencing the incentives faced by higher earners (Piketty, Saez and Stantcheva 2014), or indeed by employers. Further, fiscal policy is not simply concerned with taxes and benefits, but also with public expenditure and how it is distributed or targeted. Thus spending choices on education can directly influence inequality of opportunity.

All of the policies described above will have some influence on individual income inequality in the short run. But many of them will also influence intergenerational inequality, including the way in which wealth inequality may accumulate over time. The extent to which capital gains in housing are taxed, for example, influences the degree to which house-price rises provide an untaxed capital gain for older generations to be passed on to their descendants and thus entrench intergenerational inequality.

Although not addressing inequality directly, some economic policies may have quite profound, but unintended, effects on its evolution. For example, monetary policy is commonly the preserve of an independent central bank whose structure and remit is controlled by central government. Its decisions on interest rates and money market operations may affect asset values and therefore wealth inequality. So the Bank of England in its analysis of the effects of its quantitative easing (asset purchase) programme conducted after the financial crisis argued that:

> By pushing up a range of asset prices, asset purchases have boosted the value of households' financial wealth held outside pension funds, but holdings are heavily skewed with the top 5 per cent of households holding 40 per cent per cent of these assets. (Bell et al. 2012)

In the UK, those with the largest wealth holdings tend to live in South East England. Quantitative easing thus appears to have increased wealth inequality, both within and between the component parts of the UK.

How far can an SSG develop its own policies to combat income and/or wealth inequality? This will largely depend on its fiscal powers, since monetary policy and market regulation are generally the exclusive preserve of national governments. The extent to which fiscal powers are devolved vary significantly across countries. Thus it is difficult to generalise about the capability of SSGs to follow a different inequality strategy from central government.

Many states devolve responsibility for some parts of the taxation of physical property, although national government tends to establish broad constraints within which policy can be varied. These policies can have significant redistributive potential on both intergenerational and intragenerational inequality through their effects on property values and on inheritances.

Fiscal powers that influence the value of human assets (or capital) provide another mechanism for influencing inequality. Many SSGs control education and skills policies. Investment in education will generally take some time to influence inequality. Tuition fee policies in higher education may affect intergenerational inequality by improving the productivity of future generations. They may also reduce intragenerational inequality in the future if they are successful in attracting students from poorer backgrounds into higher education.

The extent to which policy over personal taxation and benefits is devolved to SSGs clearly varies significantly across countries. The effectiveness of such policies in addressing income inequality partly depends on the extent and design of such powers. But they may also involve trade-offs with other SSG objectives. Income taxes can be made more progressive to reduce the net income of the rich, but this may have a negative effect on economic growth if it causes workers to migrate or to reduce their working time.

Central governments generally exert some control over redistributive policies and thus provide some insurance for all citizens against adverse circumstances, irrespective of their location. To fulfil this function, they must retain control over some taxes that can be levied progressively and/or some welfare benefits or transfers that are triggered by adverse events. Such central government powers constrain the redistributive space available to SSGs. In particular, the devolution of welfare benefits to SSGs is relatively rare.

SSGs may also use moral suasion to try to reduce income inequality. Where they do not have legal powers, nevertheless they can use their influence to try to persuade organisations to adopt policies that will reduce inequality. For example, the last Scottish Government adopted a Living Wage policy and appointed a Fair Work Secretary. The purpose of these initiatives was to improve conditions for low-income workers. Employers were encouraged to pay the Living Wage, which was set significantly higher than the minimum wage. They were also encouraged to apply for accreditation as a Living Wage employer, with the Scottish Government arguing that accreditation would bring benefits such as higher productivity to the company. This shows how an SSG might use persuasion in an area where it has no legislative competence to differentiate its inequality policies from those of central government.

In the next section, we summarise evidence that we and others have accumulated about inequality in Scotland. This will provide a backdrop to discussions of policy options for Scotland.

Inequality in Scotland: what we know

Income derives from a number of sources, the largest of which is income from employment – wages. In Scotland, as in the UK, significant increases in wage inequality occurred during the 1980s, driven by a combination of deindustrialisation, financial sector deregulation, labour market deregulation and weakening of labour market institutions (trade unions and pay bargaining arrangements). Since the 1990s, the rise in wage inequality has continued, but at a slower rate, at least in part thanks to the introduction of the minimum wage in 1997 (Butcher, Dickens and Manning 2012). However, although the rise in overall wage inequality has slowed, changes in the pattern of inequality have become more nuanced. Weekly wage inequality among males has increased due to large increases in the variance of hours worked and an increase in part-time working. Rising educational attainment has mitigated the growth in inequality to an extent, but there has been an increase in wage inequality between educational groups (Lindley and Machin 2013).

Perhaps the most notable aspect of the growth of wage inequality during the past thirty years has been the rise in the share of the total wage bill going to the highest earning 1 or 2 per cent of workers. The share of income earned by the highest earning 1 per cent in Scotland increased from 6 per cent in 1997–8 to 9 per cent in 2009–10 (Bell and Eiser 2013). The majority of this increase can be accounted for by workers in the financial industries (Bell and Eiser 2015b).

Following our previous arguments, some have attempted to explain the rise of the top 1 per cent in the context of globalisation and technological change, which widen the marketplace over which the most productive individuals can leverage their talents (Mankiw 2013). Others argue that the rise of the top 1 per cent can be explained by a range of market and policy failures which allow exploitation of monopoly power, rent-seeking by CEOs and failures in corporate pay-setting, and the exercise of political influence (Piketty, Saez and Stantcheva 2014; Stiglitz 2015). From a policy perspective, one clear implication of this is that income tax revenues have become increasingly concentrated on a narrow base. The highest earning 1 per cent of taxpayers accounted for 20 per cent of Scottish income tax liabilities in 2009–10, and this figure seems likely to have increased since then (Miller and Pope 2016).

The system of personal taxation and welfare benefits mitigates market (pre-tax and benefit) income inequality. Until 2015–16, these systems were effectively common throughout the UK. Changes to these taxes and benefits had broadly the same effects on Scotland as they did in other parts of the UK. Thus, during the 1980s, substantial real reductions in spending on social protection (including benefits for those out of work, the disabled and pensioners), combined with reductions in the top rates of income tax, contributed to the increasing inequality of net household incomes. From the mid-1990s until the late 2000s, real increases in benefits for low-income families (through tax credits) and in the state pension stabilised net income inequality, despite increases in underlying market income inequality. Reductions in benefit rates for low-income households since 2010 have not yet led to significant increases in net income inequality, largely because of steep real wage falls following the financial crisis (and even steeper falls in self-employment earnings) across the income distribution (Belfield et al. 2015).

As discussed previously, incomes of pensioners have caught up with those of working age individuals, after taking account of housing costs. This is due to real increases in the state pension, the generosity of some defined benefit pension schemes (most of which are now closed to future pensioners) and limited wage growth among those of working age. The reduction in inequality between these age groups is a further explanation of the inertia in net income inequality.

There is some variation in inequality across the UK. Nowhere is it higher than in London, where pockets of extreme poverty and very substantial wealth coexist. Inequality in Scotland is broadly similar to that in Great Britain (excluding London) (Bell, Eiser and McGoldrick 2014). The main driver of differences in inequality between London and other parts of Great Britain lies in the higher numbers of top earners who live in the capital city. The distribution of low to median incomes shows much less variation across the UK.

Wealth data are less readily available and less reliable than data on income. However, the ONS Wealth and Assets Survey suggests that wealth is much more unequally distributed than income. In Scotland, the same survey suggests that the 75th percentile of the wealth distribution is ten times more valuable than the wealth of the 25th percentile.

The main components of wealth are housing and pensions. Housing wealth is increasingly concentrated among older people. While the rate of home ownership fell among under-35s between 1994–5 and 2011–12, it increased among older age groups and increased significantly among the over-65s (Bell, Eiser and McGoldrick 2014). Significantly, the proportion of over-65s who own their homes outright (without a mortgage) also increased markedly during this period. Pensioner households accounted for 27 per cent of owner occupied homes in 1994, rising to 43 per cent by 2013.

As wealth becomes increasingly concentrated among older generations, subsequent generations are likely to be increasingly reliant on inheritances to acquire assets. If wealth and incomes were equally distributed within the older generation, inheritances would be likely also to be equally distributed, and thus inheritances might not inhibit social mobility. With income and wealth being unequally distributed among the old, however, the concern is that inheritances magnify intra-generational inequality in subsequent generations. Indeed, although home ownership among under-35s in Scotland has fallen, the proportion of under-35s owning their home outright (as opposed to with a mortgage) has actually risen, providing suggestive evidence that inheritance is becoming increasingly important in helping younger generations get on the housing ladder.

Intragenerational inequality in Scotland is somewhat lower than in the UK as a whole, largely due to the relative scarcity of high-income earners in Scotland. However, one of us has shown (Lisenkova, Sanchez-Martinez and Sefton 2015) that intergenerational inequality is higher in Scotland than elsewhere in the UK. That is, in order to achieve intergenerational balance (a situation where future generations face the same fiscal burden as current generations), tax rates would have to rise significantly further in Scotland than in the UK as a whole. Unless these adjustments are made, the government deficit will not be eliminated even in the long run. This finding arises due to the relatively larger size of Scotland's older population and the associated pension and healthcare costs. The Scottish Government does not control institutional arrangements in the pensions industry nor the state pension and therefore has no ability to impact pension liabilities. It can influence healthcare expenditures, although the ageing of the population seems to be associated with a desire to consume more, rather than fewer, healthcare resources. The only way to close this loop is to have substantial increases in productivity in this sector, an issue that attracts little political attention in Scotland.

Lisenkova, Sanchez-Martinez and Sefton also discuss the issue of Scotland's share of UK net debt. Although net debt per person stood at £124,500 per Scottish resident in 2013 (based on a population share of the UK national debt), its importance will decline if there is a return to historic trends of productivity growth and future UK governments aim for a balanced budget. Clearly this is not a process over which the Scottish Government has any influence. Control over debt, at least as defined in the national accounts (or under the Maastricht Treaty), remains the preserve of the UK Government. The Scottish Government cannot influence that part of intergenerational inequality in Scotland that derives from the UK national debt because it has almost no power to influence that debt. The qualifier 'almost' is used because the Scotland Act (2016) confers capital borrowing powers on the Scottish Government of up to £2.2 billion from the National Loans Fund. Compared to the overall national debt, this is a relatively small sum, amounting to around £2,360 per Scottish resident. The Scottish Government can also borrow from the commercial banks or issue bonds. Use of any of these mechanisms for capital spending implies the establishment of new assets and liabilities which may benefit or disadvantage future generations. Use of borrowing to fund current spending only creates liabilities for future taxpayers.

However, the strict national accounts definition of debt excludes some classes of liability over which the Scottish Government does have control and which directly impinges on intergenerational equity. These include debts incurred by Network Rail, future liabilities being incurred by the Scottish Futures Trust and current liabilities incurred under the Public Private Partnership (PPP) initiative. The current annual servicing costs of these are £1.048 billion (Scottish Government 2015b). They are increasing and will account for around 3.7 per cent of the Scottish Government's budget in 2016–17. The Scottish Government has taken a self-denying ordinance to not let these payments exceed 5 per cent of its annual budget.

PPP spending creates assets as well as liabilities. The extent to which PPP schemes are fair or unfair to future generations depends on whether the economic and social value of the assets exceeds the stream of liabilities. The effect of the self-denying ordinance is to limit the extent to which the current generation of Scots takes decisions that affect future generations. Even though there may be occasions when such decisions would improve the well-being of future Scots, there is always a risk that changes in the technical, social or economic environment render well-intentioned capital spending by past generations redundant. Such redundancy increases intergenerational inequality by presenting future generations with liabilities but no corresponding assets.

Debt is thus one of the key channels by which government decisions affect intergenerational inequality. Fiscal powers that reduce wealth transfers between generations, such as inheritance tax, provide another source of intervention. Taxes that affect the value of assets also have a role. These include the existing range of property taxes (council tax and non-domestic rates), but also include alternatives such as land value tax. This contrasts with intragenerational inequality, where the policy debate in Scotland centres around changing the structure of income tax and of welfare benefits.

Conclusions

This chapter has attempted to show that the issue of inequality can be viewed from many valid perspectives. Inevitably, this implies that policy prescriptions for its reduction are complex and likely to be contested. Further, an historical perspective on inequality is necessary to understand some of the long-run changes that have influenced its evolution – whether these be technological, institutional or related to changing patterns of world trade. Again, these suggest that policies that result in lasting reductions in inequality without significantly jeopardising living standards are likely to take some time to have effect. They are unlikely to conform to the electoral cycle. For example, taxes on inheritance can only work as one generation replaces its predecessor. Similarly, spending policies aimed at enhancing the education and skills of those from poorer backgrounds inevitably take some time to affect wages and thereby to reduce inequality.

We have also seen that the existence of different levels of government with different powers and possibly different views about redistribution further complicates inequality policy. It is difficult to conceive of any economic or institutional policy that has no effect on the distribution of income between the rich and poor. Control over monetary policy and sufficient fiscal powers to effect some redistribution across different parts of its territory are almost defining characteristics of a nation state. These will have intended and unintended consequences for inequality. In response to the financial crisis, as we have seen, UK monetary policy probably increased wealth inequality. On the other hand, benefit payments from the UK Government offset reductions in income caused by the recession. During this period, the Scottish Government had few fiscal powers and therefore little short-term leverage over inequalities of income or of wealth. Its control over spending programmes – education, skills, etc. – might affect both intergenerational and/or intragenerational inequality, though not in the short run.

Do the new fiscal powers included in the Scotland Act (2016) provide significant new powers to combat inequality? The new tax powers include the ability to define the bands and rates of income tax and powers over income tax, a share of VAT receipts, Air Passenger Duty and the aggregates levy. Along with existing property taxes, the revenues from these taxes account for around 40 per cent of total revenues raised in Scotland. New welfare powers, worth around £2.5 billion (14 per cent of total welfare spending) and mainly focused on support for the disabled, will be transferred to Scotland sometime in the future. In addition, Scotland will have the power to create new benefits and to top up reserved benefits (see Chapter 4).

Together, these measures might seem to provide the Scottish Government with a powerful armoury with which to combat inequality. Income tax, which accounts for more than half of the additional revenue coming to Scotland, is commonly thought of as a powerful redistributive instrument. But the Scottish Government has no control over the income tax base, nor can it set the personal allowance, which are both important determinants of the progressivity of the tax. Further, changing income tax rates can only have a limited effect on inequality if the level of market inequality (spread of pre-tax incomes) is already high. Our previous analysis (Comerford and Eiser 2014) suggests that small changes to the basic and higher rates of income tax in Scotland would have only a tiny effect on inequality. Even substantial increases in the progressivity of income tax would still fail to reduce income inequality close to Scandinavian levels. Because pre-tax incomes are so unequal, plausible changes to Scotland's income tax structure have only a small effect on intragenerational inequality.

The inequality of pre-tax incomes has made total income tax revenues increasingly dependent on a relatively small number of very high earners, who are increasingly aware of their importance to Scotland's revenues. This makes politicians wary of increasing tax rates to levels that might cause high earners to move elsewhere, rearrange their tax affairs or leave the labour market. These mechanisms give high earners substantial market power, allowing them to press politicians to minimise tax increases either directly, or through third parties such as the media. Indeed, a move by the Scottish Government to a more redistributive fiscal policy would not necessarily command popular support. Our research (Bell and Eiser 2015a) has shown that Scots are no more sympathetic to redistributive measures than citizens from other parts of the UK. If a Scottish Government did introduce significantly higher income tax rates it might succeed in driving down intragenerational inequality within Scotland, but if higher tax rates reduce economic activity within

Scotland inequality may fall but the cost will be lower average incomes.

Another argument is that Scotland's new welfare powers are potentially a powerful redistributive mechanism. Even though the benefits being transferred are mainly concentrated on disability, the powers to introduce new benefits and to top up reserved benefits offer opportunities to support the incomes of poorer Scots and so reduce inequality. However, the new welfare budget will not be separate from other parts of the Scottish Government budget. Therefore, increased welfare spending implies spending less on other programmes, some of which may also be motivated by equity concerns. An alternative might be to fund new benefits from increased borrowing. However, the Scotland Act (2016) states that Scotland's borrowing powers were intended for capital spending and to maintain budgetary stability: their use to support current spending on welfare programmes was not envisaged, and indeed their size is relatively limited (£2.2 billion for capital and £500 million for budgetary stability). Substantial borrowing to support more egalitarian welfare provision seems to be impossible within current legislation. Further, those concerned with intergenerational equity might argue that although such borrowing might reduce inequality within the current generation, it would increase inequality between generations, since future generations would eventually have to repay this borrowing.

One might argue that the long-run health of the economy would be improved if, reflecting Piketty's view of the causes of inequality, high earners had less influence over the setting of their own pay. Some might argue that a return to a more graduated reward structure within firms would have both a direct effect in reducing inequality and also an indirect effect by weakening the political power of top earners. However, it is difficult to see what policies a Scottish Government might introduce to engineer such changes if the UK Government was unwilling to follow suit, given the high level of integration between the labour market in Scotland and that in the rest of the UK.

If the power of income tax to influence inequality is relatively weak due to its incentive effects, the reform of property taxation may provide a potential alternative. However, in this case, the target is wealth rather than income inequality. Land value tax, a potential replacement for council tax, is a quasi-wealth tax, which is less likely to distort productive activity than income tax (Wightman 2014). This reform of property taxation has been possible since the devolution of local government finance in the Scotland Act (1998).

Equality of opportunity can be influenced by public spending choices. A large attainment gap between pupils from the most and least deprived backgrounds has long been a concern of the Scottish Government, and will be a key focus of attention in the Fifth Parliamentary Session (2016–21). Related to this is the Scottish Government's flagship policy of free higher education (HE) tuition, which is justified on the grounds that the introduction of tuition fees would be socially divisive and discriminate against the poorest. Others argue that this perspective is disingenuous, as the commitment to universally free HE tuition has come at the cost of less generous grants and bursaries for the poorest students (Hunter-Blackburn 2014). But the HE funding debate also has important implications for intergenerational equity. Where tuition fees are funded through current taxation receipts, the burden is placed on the current generation of taxpayers. Where they are funded through government borrowing, or through the provision of loans to students of which only a proportion will be paid back in full, some element of the funding of HE tuition costs will fall on future generations.

Perceptions of inequality and fairness reflect the mores of society and are by no means constant. However, where levels of inequality are such that they impede economic efficiency (for example, by preventing social mobility) or interfere with the democratic process (for example, by giving some groups privileged access to the levers of power), then even a state that is more committed to economic growth than to reducing inequality can legitimately intervene to reduce the gap between rich and poor, or between this generation and the next. Both the UK and Scottish Governments have a range of powers that could be used to influence the evolution of inequality within Scotland. Perhaps the most influential powers have been retained by Westminster, including the design of key institutions that influence pre-tax incomes (such as the minimum wage and trade union regulation). Our discussion has shown that, whatever the level of government, interventions will be complex, will have to take account of both their political and economic ramifications, and are unlikely to reduce inequality significantly along any of its dimensions in the short run. The increase in inequality that is now the subject of much political angst evolved over a long period of time. Given the huge changes in industrial structure and trade patterns which have taken place, policy-induced reductions in inequality are likely to take a long time and will have to be embedded within an economy whose structure is quite different from that of the immediate post-war decades. Our understanding of equality and fairness will have to adapt to the realities of the modern Scottish economy and to the complexity of policies and powers at different levels of government that will determine its course.

4 Towards a Fairer Scotland? Assessing the Prospects and Implications of Social Security Devolution

Nicola McEwen

When the SNP first assumed office in 2007, creating a wealthier and fairer Scotland became one of the Scottish Government's five core strategic objectives. Its main aim was to support wealth generation and 'allow more people to share fairly in that wealth' through improved employment opportunities and effective public service delivery (Scottish Government 2016a). The 'fairness' agenda has increased in significance and profile since Nicola Sturgeon became First Minister. Her programme for government included the core commitment 'to use new powers to improve the welfare system, mitigating some of the worst impacts of the UK Government's cuts' (Scottish Government 2015c). The link back to the UK social security system reveals both the political opportunity and institutional complexity created by the partial devolution of social security contained within the Scotland Act (2016).

The Scottish Parliament already controls substantial areas of the welfare state. Legislative and executive competence over health, housing, education and social care were all transferred as part of the original devolution settlement. But for Scotland, as for Wales, social security remained reserved to Westminster, and although it was devolved in Northern Ireland, the parity principle and corresponding Treasury subvention was expected to ensure a single social security and benefits system for citizens across the UK. Devolution increased differences in the UK welfare state, but the social security system remained largely intact. By 2012, this integrated system had begun to unravel in the context of controversial UK welfare reforms, amid growing demands for distinctive welfare approaches across the UK's nations and regions. The Scottish independence referendum was set against the backdrop of debates over the capacity of UK welfare to reflect social solidarity and provide adequate social protection. In response to the welfare reforms and cuts to social security imposed by the UK Government, pro-independence campaigners argued that solidarity could best be preserved and reinforced if the Scottish Government had full powers to enable them to develop a Nordic-style welfare system. The Scottish Government had already introduced policies to mitigate some of the effects of welfare cuts, most notably in the introduction and expansion of discretionary housing payments to counteract the infamous 'bedroom tax'. Similarly, the Scottish Welfare Fund replaced the discretionary UK Social Fund, providing community care and crisis grants to those most in need.

These early interventions into the social security sphere are small compared to the scope and opportunity of the new social security powers in the Scotland Act (2016). They include a transfer of competence over benefits equating to around £2.7 billion, or 15.3 per cent of current social security spending in Scotland (Scottish Government 2016b). These are mainly benefits for people with disabilities, carers and non-contributory benefits for the elderly and others benefiting from the regulated Social Fund. Additional flexibility is also to be permitted in the delivery of the Universal Credit, the UK Government's flagship integrated social security and tax credit programme for working-age claimants, including the power to change its housing component. The settlement further includes the power to 'top up' reserved benefits or to create new benefits within specified constraints. Together, these new competences create the prospect of the development of a distinctive social security regime in Scotland. Leading the consultation on a 'Fairer Scotland', the then Cabinet Secretary for Social Justice expressed his aspiration that 'new powers over social security, despite their limited scope, will provide opportunities to develop different policies for Scotland which are fairer and help tackle inequalities and poverty, in line with the core purpose of the Scottish government' (Scottish Government 2015a). Yet the limited nature of the new powers, the needs they are intended to support, and the institutional, financial and cultural interdependencies that surround them may constrain the extent to which such aspirations can be fulfilled.

This chapter examines the extent to which this partial rescaling of social security enhances the capacity of the Scottish

Government to achieve its strategic goal of creating a fairer and more equal Scotland. It first explores the purposes of social security, as well as the opportunities and risks associated with decentralising or federalising social security across multiple government scales. It then examines in more detail the scope of social security devolution in Scotland, and considers the opportunities these powers create for the development and strengthening of a distinctive welfare regime in Scotland, and the complexities and challenges arising from the package of devolved powers which may affect the government's capacity to achieve its strategic goals. It concludes that the nature and interdependencies of the devolution settlement, as well as the demographic and financial challenges that face all governments, will pose obstacles that the Scottish Government will have to navigate in its pursuit of fairness.

Rescaling social security

The development of the welfare state was widely regarded as having reinforced the *nation* state, by enhancing the authority and legitimacy of central government. States acquired powers to intervene in the lives of their citizens, to equip the population for the demands of the industrial era, to modify the detrimental effects of market forces, to provide minimum standards of living and social care, and to promote social cohesion (Esping-Andersen 1999; Mishra 1999; Briggs 2000). These services were provided within bounded polities, strengthening the ties that bind citizens to the state (Tilly 1996; Ferrera 2005). They reinforced the social contract between citizen and state – the exchange of social rights and obligations shared by virtue of one's membership of the nation state (Marshall 1950). That contract was not only vertical, between citizen and state, but built upon and generated a sense of mutual belonging and obligation among fellow citizens such that – to varying, ideologically contested degrees – citizens made contributions in the knowledge that these may be redistributed to fellow citizens most in need.

The idea of a social contract is especially evident in the field of social security. Social security provides insurance, in the form of cash benefits, in the face of those social contingencies which prevent citizens from maintaining an adequate standard of living solely from labour market participation. These social contingencies may relate to age, parental responsibility, disability, sickness or injury, unemployment or low pay. As well as income maintenance and replacement to protect adults and their families from the vagaries of the market, social security systems, to varying degrees, were designed to serve poverty alleviation or eradication, social cohesion, wealth redistribution, and to support a stable, productive workforce and sustained economic growth (Esping-Andersen 1999: 37; Bonoli 2007: 495).

In their early years, provisions for social insurance and protection were highly localised, provided by parishes, municipalities, charities and societies. The extension of the welfare state in the post-war period led to a shift away from local agencies and actors in the design and financing of social insurance, reducing their role to that of service providers. In the context of post-war welfare expansion, providing social protection against life's contingencies increasingly became the responsibility of central authorities, generating greater standardisation of benefits across state territories (Ferrera 2005: 54). Even in federal states where provinces formally retained constitutional competence over social security (as in Canada), the spending and tax powers of federal governments facilitated welfare nationalisation, to ensure at least a minimum standard of benefits through the provision of state-wide social security programmes and conditional fiscal transfers (Obinger, Leibfried and Castles 2005).

Such centralisation gave states the capacity to foster and reinforce social citizenship, the 'continuing series of transactions between persons and agents of a given state in which each has enforceable rights and obligations' by virtue of their shared citizenship status (Tilly 1996: 8; see also Marshall 1950). Where they had the will to do so, central governments could also harness their powers over social security to promote social cohesion and solidarity between class and territorial communities within the state. The introduction of obligatory social insurance played an important role in state- and nation-building, allowing states to establish themselves as powerful vehicles for redistribution 'capable of affecting the life chances of millions of citizens ... and providing highly concrete manifestations of that process of institutional differentiation vis-à-vis foreign spaces' (Ferrera 2005: 55). Ferrera argued that aligning redistributive boundaries with the territorial boundaries of the state reinforced the distinction between citizens and outsiders, thus helping to forge commonality and a sense of mutual belonging among fellow citizens. Within multinational states like Canada, the UK and Belgium, where state and national boundaries do not coincide and there are multiple communities of belonging, the capacity of the central state to provide for the social and economic security of its citizens helped to strengthen citizens' loyalty to existing state structures. State social protection also helped to stave off nationalist and secessionist demands, by heightening the risks and potential losses that could be incurred by major constitutional change (McEwen 2006).

From the 1970s, as systems were stretched by inflation, lower levels of economic growth and rising levels of unemployment, the purposes and mechanisms of social security began to shift. The language of 'new social risks' emerged to describe changing economic and socio-demographic structures of a post-industrial society, challenging traditional mechanisms of social protection (Taylor-Gooby 2004: 2–3). Growing income inequality meant that work could no longer guarantee an escape from poverty, while the growth in social security spending faced by all advanced democratic states generated pressures to curtail costs. Labour market instability, the problem of long-term unemployment and underemployment, the ageing population and its effect on dependency ratios and caring responsibilities, the entry of women into the labour force and changes in the traditional family structure have all placed strains on social security systems, leading to processes of restructuring and reform (Pierson 2001; Bonoli 2007). In response, many states have reduced the scope of benefit entitlement, and transitioned from universality towards more selective, means-tested benefits. There has also been a general trend from 'passive' to 'active' labour market policies, with a greater association between the entitlement to benefits and the obligation of benefit claimants to meet certain conditions of job-seeking or training in an effort to reduce long-term dependency and to ensure their reinsertion into the labour market (Ferrera and Rhodes 2000: 4–5). As well as weakening social solidarity across class groups, these changes undermine the capacity of the state to maintain interregional solidarity, and nationalist movements have used the language of welfare and social solidarity to advance their autonomy demands (McEwen 2006; Béland and Lecours 2008; Vampa 2014). The gradual Europeanisation of social security entitlements may have further undermined the social contract between the citizens and the central state. By giving precedence to the social security entitlements of EU workers and residents irrespective of their nationality, EU regulations and court rulings have contributed to decoupling social rights and obligations from national citizenship (Ferrera 2005: 49).

The retreat from state welfare has coincided with the rise of regional authority. In advanced democratic states, many new elected regional legislatures and governments have either been established or existing regional institutions have acquired increased powers and responsibilities (Keating 1998; Hooghe, Marks and Schakel 2008). Regional institutions now make legislative, policy and spending decisions over a vast range of activities central to their populations, including over many areas of welfare. This has led to a divergence in social citizenship rights and public service provision such that in multilevel states, there isn't a single *national* welfare system, but distinctive welfare regimes, with rights and responsibilities dependent upon where in the country one lives (Jeffery 2002; McEwen and Moreno 2005; Gallego and Subirats 2012).

There is widespread debate within the literature on the effects of decentralising welfare. For some, the increased vulnerability of sub-state nations and regions to capital and middle-class flight can make their governments reluctant to pursue progressive welfare where it would involve imposing a higher tax burden on high earners or curtailing market flexibility (Huber, Ragin and Stephens 1993; Swank 2002; Rodden 2003; Obinger, Leibfried and Castles 2005). Conversely, support for generous and redistributive welfare systems may be more easily maintained at the sub-state level, where a shared sense of solidarity and mutual belonging is often stronger. Greater institutional thickness between government, the business community, the trade unions and the third sector may also help to forge a sense of common purpose and willingness to compromise to achieve shared goals (Moreno 2003; McEwen 2006; Keating 2009). Moreover, decentralisation can stimulate social policy innovation, with sub-state governments acting as a locus of policy experimentation, with successes emulated by others (Banting 2005; Gallego and Subirats 2012).

Notwithstanding the decentralising trend, the welfare competences of sub-state governments tend to be weighted more towards public service delivery, for example in health, education, social housing, social and childcare, or social assistance.

Central and federal governments continue to retain greater competences in employment-related social insurance and social protection, though in multinational states in particular the centre's authority in this sphere is often contested. Nonetheless, there are complex interdependencies between different elements of welfare provision which can shape and constrain policy options for government at all territorial scales. These will be explored in the Scottish context below.

Social security and devolution

When the Scottish Parliament was established it had legislative power over all areas not specifically reserved to the Westminster parliament within the Scotland Act (1998). The new parliament and government thus assumed responsibility and power over significant areas of the welfare state, including in health, education, housing and social care. However, the reservation of social security and most tax policies meant that the capacity to shape redistributive welfare remained principally with the UK Government and Parliament.

The division between devolved and reserved competencies created interdependencies in social provision, for example between housing and housing benefit, or social care and disability benefits. However, in the early years of devolution, when the Scottish and UK Governments were led by the same party (albeit in coalition in Scotland), shared similar ideological preferences and governed within a benign fiscal climate which saw steady increases in fiscal transfers to Scotland, the edges between reserved and devolved competence did not appear especially jagged. Jagged edges became more exposed when the Conservative-led coalition government embarked upon its programme of welfare reforms. These were intended to simplify the social security system, reduce the welfare burden and to promote (through cuts and curtailing entitlements) an ideologically-driven reduction in the state's responsibility for social security for working-age adults, with direct and indirect consequences for devolved competence. For the first time since its establishment, the devolved legislature refused to grant legislative consent to those aspects of the Welfare Reform Bill which cut directly across devolved competence, and the Scottish Parliament embarked upon its own welfare journey. A new

Welfare Reform Committee was established to monitor the implementation of UK welfare reform in Scotland, and to consider relevant Scottish legislation, including scrutinising the Scottish Government's first foray into social security (Welfare Reform Committee 2016).

Following the UK Government's termination and subsequent devolution (with a 10 per cent cut) of responsibility for the discretionary Social Fund, the Scottish Government set up its own, more generous Scottish Welfare Fund to give grants to those in crisis or in need of community care. It introduced discretionary housing payments to mitigate the effects of the removal of what the UK Government deemed to be a 'spare room subsidy' given to those living in social housing in receipt of housing benefit (otherwise known as the bedroom tax). Notwithstanding these early measures in social security devolution, the Scotland Act (2016) represents a step change in devolved competence in this sphere (UK Parliament 2016).

The new powers and responsibilities come in various forms. First are the range of benefits which are specifically devolved to the Scottish Parliament, including: benefits for people with disabilities and industrial injuries; Attendance Allowance; Carer's Allowance; the Regulated Social Fund; Sure Start maternity grants; funeral grants; cold weather payments; and winter fuel payments – see Figure 4.1. The Scottish Parliament will have the legislative autonomy to alter the level and scope of these benefits, to withdraw them, or to replace them with an alternative benefit or benefits serving a similar purpose. Allocated spending on these benefits at the point of implementation of the legislation will be added to the Scottish block grant, with annual adjustments according to the formula agreed within the fiscal framework.

Second are the flexibilities within Universal Credit, which will enable the Scottish Parliament to pass regulations to effect changes to its delivery (to whom and how frequently it is paid) and to the level of the housing component. This latter element would provide the Scottish Government with a mechanism for bringing an effective end to the bedroom tax, as well as other adjustments to the housing element, such as eligible rent and local housing allowances. The Scottish Government will be required to consult the UK Secretary of State on the 'practicability' of implementing these regulations, but following a UK Government Report Stage amendment, the Secretary of State

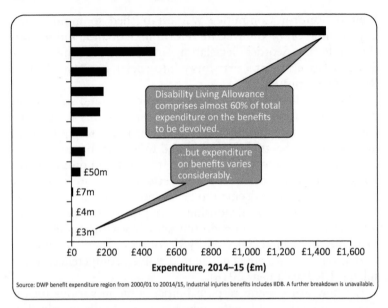

Figure 4.1 Benefit expenditure in Scotland, 2014–15.

Source: Scottish Government 2016c.

will not be able to veto Scottish regulations, only postpone their date of implementation. To do so, he/she would be required to amend the regulations by Statutory Instrument, specifying the new date of implementation. These new powers are specifically linked to the Universal Credit.

Third is the devolution of power to introduce discretionary payments enabling the Scottish Parliament to provide additional financial assistance to those already entitled to receive a reserved benefit, so long as that assistance is for at least one of the purposes served by the benefit, and is not compensation for reduction in entitlement caused by benefit sanctions imposed by the UK Department for Work and Pensions (DWP). Discretionary payments may be used to provide short-term assistance to those in particular need. Future Scottish governments will now also have an opportunity to 'top up' the level of UK benefits, for example, to offset the effects of a UK Government decision to cut or freeze the level of benefits, or to boost the level of support offered to benefit recipients for groups identified as a key priority. Discretionary housing payments which are formally devolved in the Scotland Act had already been devolved by Statutory Instrument, and have been used to enable the Scottish Government to counteract the UK Government decision to remove the 'spare room subsidy' from some recipients of housing benefit.

Potentially the most radical social security provision within the Scotland Act is the power to create new benefits (UK Parliament 2016: clause 28). This provision was introduced late into the legislative process, and is much broader in scope than the 'top-up' clause. It opens up the opportunity for the Scottish Parliament to occupy space vacated by the UK Parliament (for example as a result of entitlement constraints or withdrawal of a benefit), or to introduce a new benefit in line with Scottish policy priorities. These broad powers create a further exception to the social security reservation in the Scotland Act (1998) – the original devolution settlement – by providing the Scottish Parliament with the power to create benefits, allowances, grants, loans and any other form of financial assistance *for social security purposes*, within prescribed parameters. Any new Scottish benefits must be supported from the Scottish Consolidated Fund (the Scottish Government's budget); not already devolved by other clauses within the Act; not connected to other reserved matters (other than social security); not targeted at those who would qualify by virtue of old age; and not offered where the requirement for assistance has arisen as a result of benefit sanctions. Drawing on the definitions set out in the original devolution legislation, this means that the Scottish Government could, provided it had the financial means and the political will, create new welfare benefits to those who would qualify by reason of survivorship, disability, sickness, incapacity, injury, unemployment, low income, maternity or the care of children or others needing care. For example, in light of the UK Government's intention to withdraw entitlement to housing benefit (the housing element of Universal Credit) from under-21s from 2017, the Scottish Government could introduce a Scottish youth benefit to meet this need. Or, if the Government could devise a benefit that might help it to reduce educational inequality – an issue on which Nicola Sturgeon has staked her reputation – the legislation suggests they would have the legal scope to do so.

These powers mark a significant addition to the Scottish Parliament's powers in what has hitherto been a core policy area reserved to the UK Parliament. It would be an exaggeration to suggest that they mark an end to UK-wide social security. Substantial areas of social security remain reserved, amounting to around 85 per cent of current social security spending in Scotland (Scottish Government 2016c). These include politically symbolic benefits like the State Pension (which accounts for around half of all social security spending), Child Benefit and those income-related benefits and tax credits within the Universal Credit. Moreover, the package of devolved powers remains focused on passive social security – they do not reflect the broader transitions in European systems of welfare which give pre-eminence to active labour market policies. The Smith Commission – the cross-party commission which made the recommendations upon which the new powers are based – had recommended devolution of 'all powers over support for unemployed people through the employment programmes currently contracted by DWP' (Smith Commission 2014: para. 57). This ambiguous recommendation was interpreted to mean devolving programmes to support those at risk of long-term unemployment (the Work Programme) and employment support for people with disabilities. The impact of this devolution has been rendered less meaningful still by the fact that it is to be accompanied by a cut of over 75 per cent, as the DWP shifts its emphasis towards supporting those in the early weeks and months of unemployment (Scottish Parliament Information Centre 2016).

Nonetheless, in constitutional terms, the powers are extensive. Taken together, the package of welfare-related powers within the new devolution settlement establishes social security (excluding pensions) as a concurrent competence, enabling the UK and Scottish Governments to legislate in the same social security space, and for similar purposes.

Social security devolution and a fairer Scotland

While critical of the constitutional constraints and limitations of social security devolution, the SNP government has also been keen to talk up the opportunities it creates. Setting out the Government's vision of social security as being 'important to all of us and able to support each of us when we need it', the then Cabinet Secretary for Social Justice, Communities and Pensioners' Rights claimed the new powers offered 'a real opportunity, over time, to make Scotland a fairer country' (Scottish Government 2016d: 3). An early move was to change the terminology, adopting the term 'social security' over 'welfare' in an attempt to rediscover a system derived from social citizenship entitlements and avoid the stigmatisation associated with a conception of social security as a societal burden providing relief for the poor. This provides some evidence to suggest a greater willingness, and perhaps ability, to capture social solidarity at the Scottish level, reinforcing the collectivist and *national* purpose of social security. More substantive changes, however, will have to be considered alongside a variety of bureaucratic, institutional, demographic and financial constraints.

Irrespective of constitutional capacity, the institutions for the delivery of welfare shape the level of effective autonomy that can be exercised. Unlike the DWP, the Scottish Government is not a delivery agency – it does not deliver public services directly but works with a range of public sector and third sector partners (health boards, local authorities, charities) to provide services financed by and in accordance with Scottish policy and legislative commitments. The Smith Report left open the option of whether the Scottish Government should develop its own welfare bureaucracy to deliver new devolved benefits, such as Personal Independence Payments (PIPs) and Attendance Allowance, or whether it should negotiate a contract with the DWP to act as an agent to deliver devolved benefits on its behalf. Both options would have incurred a cost, though the former can be expected to be more costly and require more time to set up new systems. The latter would have made it difficult technically (given IT infrastructure, personnel and delivery systems) to develop benefits for Scotland that were markedly different from the benefits that the DWP delivers for England and Wales.

After an intensive period of consultation with a very broad range of stakeholders, the Scottish Government announced its intention to set up its own welfare bureaucracy in the form of a new executive agency to oversee policy implementation and the delivery of devolved benefits. This was selected after appraising the strengths and weaknesses of a range of alternatives. These included negotiating a Service Level Agreement with the DWP or another body outside Scotland (such as the Northern Ireland Security Agency), outsourcing by procurement, expanding the functions of an existing Scottish national or local public sector body, or creating a Scottish Government core directorate to deliver benefits directly. Each was assessed on the basis of the ease of organisation and level of control it afforded, issues of governance and accountability, flexibility in delivering Scottish policy models, affordability, practicability and alignment with other delivery mechanisms, services and data sources (Scottish Government 2016e).

Intriguingly, the decision to set up a new agency is a bolder move than the plans laid down for the transition to independence prior to the referendum. Then, the SNP government accepted the recommendation of its Expert Working Group on Welfare to negotiate a shared bureaucracy for an unspecified transitional period. The Expert Group believed that 'formalizing the current [bureaucratic] arrangements into an agreed set of "shared services" would safeguard delivery, as well as being the most efficient and cost effective arrangement for both governments, in a period of transition' (Expert Working Group on Welfare 2013: 44). That recommendation was, of course, made with reference to a transition to independence, which would have signalled a far more comprehensive and complex transfer of powers and responsibilities than is the case here. Nonetheless, the Expert Group identified some of the bureaucratic interdependencies in UK social security, which may prove challenging in a transition to a new Scottish delivery agency. For example, Scotland-based claims for Disability Living Allowance (DLA), one of the benefits being devolved, are currently processed at Disability Benefit Centres in Scotland, England and Wales, while the Glasgow Disability Centre also processes claims from some English postal districts. Another of the devolved benefits, Attendance Allowance, is administered for the whole of the UK from offices in Preston and Blackpool (Expert Working Group on Welfare 2013: 48–9). This foretells some challenges in building capacity within Scotland and negotiating the possible transfer of staff and expertise.

The Scottish Government is only required, by statute, to cooperate with the UK Government in relation to the Universal Credit provisions, but the interaction between reserved UK benefits and Scottish devolved benefits will create a need for more extensive cooperation between the two governments. There have always been jagged edges between devolved and reserved competence in the social sphere. These were exposed when the Scottish Parliament refused to grant legislative consent to the

UK Welfare Reform Bill for its consequential effects on the eligibility to key passported benefits and services in Scotland, such as blue-badge parking and legal aid, for which receipt of a UK benefit is assumed as a proxy measure for needs related to low income or disability. Likewise, entitlement to some benefits which are to be devolved under the Scotland Act (2016) serves as a passport to other benefits and services, many of which are reserved. PIPs, for example, act as a passport to a range of reserved benefits and services, including disability premiums in Housing Benefit, disability elements of Working Tax Credits and exemptions from or deductions to Vehicle Excise Duty, among others. Any changes in eligibility criteria for PIPs after devolution, or a change in the nature of the benefit, would therefore have a knock-on effect for UK Government spending on reserved benefits. Some reserved benefits are paid net of income tax. If the Scottish Government changed income tax rates or bands which led to increased (or decreased) individual or household income after tax, this could decrease (or increase) UK Government spending on means-tested benefits. These interactions are likely to augment the complexities of the benefit system over time if, as expected, the two systems diverge.

The 'no detriment' principles set out within the Smith Commission Report both reflect and intensify institutional interdependence. These principles were intended to ensure that: (1) neither government suffers financial detriment as a result of the decision to transfer new powers and responsibilities; and (2) neither government suffers financial detriment as a result of the policy decisions of the other after devolution (Smith Commission 2014). The reverse should also hold; each government should get the full benefit from its own policy decisions. The fiscal framework agreement, reached after eleven months of intense negotiation between the Scottish and UK Governments, set out how the 'no detriment' principles will be interpreted and operationalised (HM Government/Scottish Government 2016). In relation to policy spillovers, it draws a distinction between direct effects and behavioural effects. The former concern the financial effects that 'directly and mechanically' arise from the policy change. An example would be where changes in the eligibility criteria of a devolved disability benefit increase UK Government spending on those benefits and services to which that disability benefit acts as a passport. The latter refer to financial effects resulting from changes in individual or household behaviour following a change in policy. The fiscal framework agreement includes a commitment to provide recompense for all direct spillover effects. Only in exceptional circumstances will behavioural effects involving 'a material and demonstrable welfare cost or saving' be taken into account. But both governments will have to agree with the evidence establishing causality before any fiscal transfer or compensation is made. The operation of 'no detriment' rules will require ongoing auditing, oversight, negotiation and even mediation, with the obvious potential for intergovernmental dispute and stalemate.

It is not yet clear how these interdependencies will be managed. The Joint Ministerial Working Group on Welfare was established in February 2015 to provide a forum for discussion and decision making to support the implementation of the welfare-related aspects of the new devolution settlement. It met four times in its first year, supported by regular communication and strong cooperative working between officials in the Scottish Government and the DWP. However, political differences and competing agendas may disrupt intergovernmental cooperation. The Joint Exchequer Committee (JEC), upon which the Joint Ministerial Working Group on Welfare is loosely modelled, was initially set up to oversee implementation of the Scotland Act (2012), but did not meet at all between 2013 and 2015 when political disagreements surfaced.[1]

Demographic and fiscal constraints

The demographic and financial challenges that have faced all welfare states are just as evident at the sub-state level. Sub-state governments must also confront new social risks, including from demographic changes such as an ageing population. As discussed above, they may be especially vulnerable to the prospect of the flight of higher earners upon whose income they depend to deliver social welfare and other public services. These challenges are especially evident within the context of social security devolution.

The bulk of those benefits being devolved to Scotland apply to older Scots, people with disabilities or carers. For the most part, these groups are economically inactive and dependent upon the state for social and financial support and, indirectly, the contributions of economically active citizens. Demographic trends point towards some challenges in meeting needs over the medium to long term. Although projecting future demographic trends is notoriously difficult, the Scottish Government's own projections point towards an increase in the proportion of those who may require devolved social security relative to those contributing to supporting their needs. Amid a projection of a general increase in the population of Scotland, the number of people of pensionable age and over is projected to rise from 1.06 million in 2014 to 1.36 million by 2039 – an increase of around 28 per cent.[2] Over the same period, the number of people aged 75 and over is projected to increase by around 29 per cent by 2024, and by 85 per cent by 2039, to 0.8 million in 2039. Not all of those will be in need of social security from the Scottish Government. The biggest social security pressures will fall on the state pension, which under the new constitutional settlement remains wholly the responsibility of the UK Government.

These older citizens, however, may be expected to increase the cost pressures on other areas of devolved services, most notably health and social care. At the same time, the 'dependency ratio' – the ratio of children and pensioners to those of working age – is projected to rise from around 58 dependants per 100 working population in 2014 to 67 per 100 in 2039 (National Records Office 2015). Since the former tend to be less economically active and more dependent on the state for financial and social support than those who are of working age, these projected demographic trends suggest that Scottish governments of the future may have to find ways to generate additional revenue to meet existing spending needs, limiting the scope for significant welfare expansion.

Further financial pressures will emerge from the system of territorial finance. UK social security is normally supported according to need. So, spending by the DWP is mainly categorised as Annually Managed Expenditure (AME), and represents the actual costs of providing benefits for which entitlement is set by the UK Government. The parity principle ensures a similar system of financing social security in Northern Ireland. By contrast, when the Scottish block grant is adjusted to account for additional social security responsibilities, it will not be based on actual social security spending in Scotland, or an evaluation of spending needs. Instead, the social security transfers from the UK Treasury to the Scottish Government will be treated in the same way as the rest of the Scottish block grant. Application of the Barnett formula means that changes to Scottish social security transfers will be according to a proportionate share of changes to equivalent spending in England and Wales. On the one hand, this frees the Scottish Government and Parliament to develop policies as they see fit, without having to conform to UK policy. From an autonomy perspective, this contrasts favourably with the Northern Ireland model, where despite devolution, social security policies are expected to conform to UK policy in exchange for the UK Government providing transfers to meet the actual costs of social security in full. On the other hand, the Scottish Government will still face the financial consequences of UK welfare policy. Where UK policy restricts entitlement to welfare benefit or withdraws a benefit equivalent to those which have been devolved to the Scottish Parliament, the social security component of the Scottish block grant will also be reduced. Moreover, this system of financing means that the Scottish Government will not be compensated for any asymmetric shocks which produce heightened demand for social security spending in Scotland but not in England and Wales.

Social security devolution coincides with the transfer of competence over the rates and thresholds of income tax. Aside from the personal allowance which remains a reserved power, from April 2017 the Scottish Government will have the responsibility for raising revenues from 100 per cent of earned income from those for whom Scotland is their main residence (Chapter 2). Some studies have suggested that decentralisation of welfare is likely to have a detrimental effect on welfare provision in territories where responsibility for revenue-raising is also decentralised, as a result of the risks of the flight of middle-class earners discussed above (Rodden 2003; Obinger, Leibfried and Castles 2005). There are many reasons to assume that an increased tax burden would not produce a mass exodus – for example, family and community ties, favourable costs of living, better public service provision and quality of life may be sufficient to offset the effects of a higher tax burden. However, there are constraints within the new devolution settlement which could heighten the risks of increasing revenues to support progressive welfare, to offset cuts in fiscal transfers, or to extend redistributive taxation to serve the goal of a fairer Scotland. Not all of these involve higher earners leaving Scotland. Tax devolution applies only to earned income; taxes on unearned income, including savings and dividends, remain reserved. This leaves open the possibility that introducing a more redistributive tax system by increasing tax rates for higher earners could see this tax-savvy section of the population shift more of their income into non-devolved savings or dividends. These complexities have contributed to a cautious approach to taxation on the part of the Scottish Government (Scottish Government 2016f).

Conclusion: towards a fairer Scotland?

There are, then, significant caveats, challenges and constraints facing the Scottish Government in exercising its new social security powers. Bureaucratic challenges, constitutional complexities, demographic pressures and limitations on revenue-raising capacity may all restrict the extent to which these new powers can fulfil the goal of creating a fairer, more equal Scotland. But that is not to suggest that the new powers are meaningless to this endeavour. New powers – combined with existing powers – can make a difference.

Indeed, some of the opportunities emerge from the constraints. First, the lack of intergovernmental coordination to manage the interface between devolved and reserved powers in the social sphere has been a source of frustration for many. The new settlement creates an opportunity, as well as a need, for better and more effective coordination between governments. The early efforts in this regard seem promising, with regular meetings of the Joint Ministerial Working Group on Welfare and close and collaborative working among officials of both the UK and Scottish Governments. Rescaling social security may bring its own advantages.

Second, economies of scale suggest that it ought to be easier to develop a system for the delivery of welfare benefits in Scotland that would be simpler, more efficient and more accessible from a citizen and user perspective. That alone could address some of the biggest problems in the current system, for example, when vulnerable people dependent on disability benefits face delays in receiving benefits as a result of bureaucratic complexity and inefficiency. The best way to design a system which is responsive to the needs of those who will depend on it is to involve them in the design process as early as possible, and to develop and nurture relationships with the third sector and employers who will be key to effective policy implementation and uptake. This, too, should be easier within Scotland than it is across the UK, because of the advantages of scale, and the established culture of partnership working between the Scottish Government and its stakeholders. The Scottish Parliament Welfare Reform Committee heard witness testimony, through its 'Your Say' initiative, from those directly affected by welfare reform, and similar initiatives could help to inform the policy process and contribute to the design of a service tailored to those who rely upon it.

The Scottish Government understandably prioritised secure transition in the devolution of social security powers, to ensure that those in receipt of UK benefits do not experience disruption in payments as powers are transferred. In the short to medium term, this suggests continuity in the policies and programmes to be devolved, with perhaps some tinkering at the edges, as seen, for example, in the SNP manifesto pledge to increase the level of Carer's Allowance. In the longer term, however, there is an opportunity to expand horizons, and to learn from social security systems around the world. In particular, the new devolved social security powers over disability benefits or Attendance Allowance run parallel to existing devolved competence in social care. Notwithstanding the difficulties in confronting the interests of, and advocates for, those already in receipt of a benefit, there should be scope for reassessing whether the current balance in delivery and spending between already devolved services and soon to be devolved benefits is optimal. Further opportunities emerge from the capacity to create new benefits which may be linked to Scottish policy priorities. For example, the SNP manifesto made a commitment to restore housing benefit for 18–21-year-olds when this is cut by the UK Government, which it could do by creating a new Scottish benefit (Scottish National Party 2016: 20). The Scottish Government is considering introducing a Young Carer's Allowance alongside other measures to provide greater support to children with caring responsibilities who are currently not entitled to Carer's Allowance. These and other social security measures could make at least a small contribution to tackling inequality. But the pursuit of a fairer, more equal society can't be achieved through social security alone. It will require commitment, investment and action across a much wider range of public policies.

Notes

1. The lack of JEC meetings during that period was related to the stalemate in the negotiations between the two governments over the mechanism for block grant adjustment as a result of the transfer of new powers in the Scotland Act (2012), underlining the importance of politics over procedure.
2. This is not however projected to be a linear trend. The ONS statistics point to a slight decrease up to 2020, before rising in subsequent years.

5 A More Gender-Equal Scotland? Childcare Policy in Scotland after the Independence Referendum

Craig McAngus and Kirstein Rummery

Introduction

During the independence referendum campaign, childcare policy became a key and salient issue in the debate. The Scottish Government (2013) used its White Paper on Scottish independence to argue the case that childcare policy would improve under independence and would be part of an overall strategy to grow the Scottish economy. What was largely missing from the debate was how childcare could become part of a wider infrastructure investment to help foster a more gender-equal society in Scotland. Childcare provision has been a devolved competence since 1999, but the devolution of the income tax bands and rates opens up the potential for additional capacity in childcare to provide for an increase in the number of hours worked by parents, mostly mothers. Although childcare in Scotland does differ from childcare provision elsewhere in the UK in some important respects, the mixed model approach with a predominance of the private sector is common to both Scotland and the rest of the UK. Funding of childcare is predominantly 'demand side', meaning that parents are subsidised through the social security system rather than the bulk of investment going into providing the services themselves.

During the independence referendum, the Scottish Government's (2013) White Paper outlined that, in an independent Scotland, a more 'Nordic', supply-side approach would be adopted in order to boost maternal employment levels and thus generate higher income tax yields. Scotland voted No to independence, but the Scottish Government has remained committed to investing in childcare services. Much of the Scottish Government's arguments around childcare during the referendum centred on the notion that any increase in revenues generated as a result of increased provision would not accrue to Scotland. However, near full devolution of income tax is imminent and there now exists an incentive for the Scottish Government to reform Scotland's childcare system towards a supply-side model.

The purpose of this chapter is twofold. First, an overview of the literature on childcare policy presents a picture of which policy routes are best suited for the promotion of a more gender equal society. Second, the chapter outlines the opportunities and constraints that now exist following the devolution of further powers to Scotland for the furthering of gender equality.

Gender equality and childcare

First, we should examine why Scotland might want to extend its childcare provision. Currently, as part of the UK, Scotland is ranked ninth in Europe for gender equality using the European Gender Equality Index (Platenga et al. 2009), although it has relatively low levels of workforce and political participation by women. In OECD measures, the UK currently has the highest gap between female employment rates (76.2 per cent) and maternal employment rates (65.1 per cent) (OECD 2016). It is estimated that this shortfall costs the UK around £23 billion per annum (Rake 2000).

There is therefore a strong case to make that if the Scottish Government wishes Scotland to become more economically productive then it needs to enable more mothers to work, and work more hours. Moreover, as Scotland is a high labour-intensity market, which employs high numbers of women, it would boost employment, particularly employment of low- to middle-income women for whom the affordability of childcare is a major factor in maternal underemployment; over half of non-working mothers claim that they would engage in the labour market if they were able to gain access to affordable, high-quality childcare (Bryson, Kazimirski and Southwood 2006). Not only does boosting employment in this sector of the population address gender inequality, it also plays a significant role in stimulating local economies (Elson, Balakrishnan and Heintz 2013), as women, particularly mothers, are more likely than men to spend in the local retail and service sector. The biggest benefits are seen by low- to middle-income women for whom it can make accessing the labour market at all possible.

Supporting women's labour market participation through the provision of childcare thus has the potential to yield both long-term economic benefits and greater social equality. It is the most effective way of addressing women's and children's poverty. Investment in childcare therefore means a reduction in the economic and social costs associated with long-term poverty including ill health, reduced life expectancy, use of social services and crime, as well as the direct social and economic cost of underemployment, including reduced tax revenue and a hindrance on economic growth. The costs of poverty, particularly with the devolution of some disability benefits, are increasingly falling on the Scottish Government, which already controls the healthcare and social care budget, both of which are adversely impacted by high levels of poverty. The impact on outcomes for children is more marked the earlier the intervention: pre-school programmes demonstrate a much higher return on investment than primary schooling (Heckman 2008), particularly if the provision is of high quality and pedagogical rather than simply care (OECD 2011). Providing high-quality early years education makes a significant impact on educational and economic outcomes in later life.

Stakeholders in Scotland readily identify the problems with childcare provision in Scotland, and are keen to identify how they would like to see the system changed. The referendum campaign has been recognised as a 'window of opportunity' (Kingdon 1995; Pierson 2000; Greener 2005) for advocates of change, and the issue of childcare is now a very salient issue in Scottish politics and is often a topic of heated debate between political parties. On the whole, stakeholders believe that the reliance on market forces is to the detriment of Scotland's childcare system. There is a general consensus that childcare should be funded using a supply-side model, with stakeholders often readily pointing to childcare systems in other countries. The Nordic states are often highlighted as an example of the 'ideal' childcare model. Academic research supports this position: supply-side solutions tend to lead to better-quality provision and occur in states that measure well on gender equality indexes (Van Lancker and Ghysels 2012; White and Friendly, 2012).

The Scottish Government has recognised that the current childcare system in Scotland is a barrier to women entering the job market. Childcare has risen up the political agenda in recent years, but the issue has not been framed primarily as a 'gender equality' issue. Rather, discussions of childcare policy tend to link any policy proposals with child poverty and female employment. There have been occasions, however, when leading Scottish Government figures have discussed gender equality in explicit terms. Indeed, First Minister Nicola Sturgeon has previously said that control over equalities legislation would allow an independent Scotland to tackle, more effectively, 'the deep seated gender inequalities that still hold women back' (Sturgeon 2014). Since Nicola Sturgeon has become First Minister, there have been signs that the gender equality frame may well become more prevalent over time, and there are commitments in the SNP's 2016 election manifesto, with pledges to increase childcare provision.

Childcare systems

Childcare policies can either promote traditional gender roles or encourage a more gender-equal distribution of care. Such schemes can be described as promoting 'familiasation' and 'defamiliasation' in that the can reinforce (genderise) or transform (degenderise) traditional gender roles respectively (Mischke 2011; Saxonberg 2013: 28). States that promote a dual-earner model through their family policy counteract the stress of work-family conflict in women by promoting 'role expansion' in the sense that generous childcare provision allows women to gain better life satisfaction by participating in a range of public spheres other than the home (Grönlund and Öun 2010).

The degree to which parenthood has become a crucial axis of difference between men and women varies across countries. According to Keck and Saraceno (2013: 5), family policy accounts for a significant amount of the variation, with childcare a major part of any overall policy approach (Keck and Saraceno 2013: 18). Despite the importance of childcare policy, however, there must first be 'fertile ground' in culture, values and a favourably structured job market in order for policies to encourage gender equality (Keck and Saraceno 2013: 22). Despite the best efforts of agents (governments), there are often significant structural hindrances to the achievement of gender equality that can take years or even decades to overcome.

Childcare systems similar to Scotland's often lead to a significant disjuncture between policy and service implementation as families have to access services across 'diverse economies of care' which often leads to a patchwork of care solutions (Gallagher 2013: 164). This limited access is a key reason for women not entering into the labour market (Gallagher 2013: 165). In systems that are dominated by private provision, women as consumers face numerous challenges in finding childcare (Huff and Cotte 2013: 78), and the so-called 'choice' that is offered by market solutions to policy delivery often adds stress for women and their partners (Huff and Cotte 2013: 84). Cost is often a crucial factor that will determine whether mothers think it is worthwhile re-entering the job market after parental leave (Keck and Saraceno 2013: 7). In Nordic states, childcare fees are significantly lower than in the UK and, as a result, do not act as barrier to anywhere near the same extent. Borchorst (2009) argues that childcare policy has been an explicit component in the Nordic approach to welfare provision to improve gender equality, a factor which has led these Nordic states to score consistently high in a range of gender equality indexes (for example, Plantenga et al. 2009).

The take-up of childcare services is highest in a country that promotes a coherent dual-earner family policy. In a study comparing Sweden, Finland and Germany, Krapf (2014) analyses the childcare take-up rate of these countries due to the fact that they all have extensive childcare coverage but differing family policies. Sweden, in this study, represents the country with the strongest and most coherent dual-earner approach to family policy in that there is a systematic set of policies in place to minimise the impact that having children has on mothers while, simultaneously, bringing fathers into the caring sphere (Duvander and Ferrarini 2013: 3–5).

Krapf (2014: 24) finds that Swedish children are highly likely to be in childcare regardless of the mother's family situation and education, whereas in Finland and Germany mothers with a high level of education are more likely to use childcare. Both Germany and Finland have family policy incentives for women to act as homemakers; in Sweden, there is no incentive through family policy for women to act as homemakers (Krapf 2014: 36). Van Lancker and Ghysels (2013: 28) argue that to increase equality of coverage of childcare, policy makers ought to increase supply-side provision of childcare and formulate coherent labour market and family policies so that, for example, parental leave doesn't discourage low-skilled mothers from entering the job market after long, well-paid maternity leave.

Childcare in Scotland

As it stands, Scotland's childcare provision operates on a 'mixed' model with the private, public and voluntary sectors all delivering services. Although there is a limited amount of public provision available for children from the age of three that is free at the point of use, most childcare services outside of this are paid for directly by parents and then partly subsidised through the tax credit system or vouchers from employers. According to the Family and Childcare Trust (2014: 16–17), 31 per cent of the provision of childcare in 2012 that was available for women returning to work after maternity leave, for example, is run privately and open to market forces.

One consequence of having a system that heavily relies on market forces is that provision is 'patchy', particularly in poorer and rural areas where demand is unlikely to be as high as in more affluent, urban areas. This means that the capacity to enter the job market is not the same across Scotland, and that parents who live in more affluent, urban areas have a greater choice of services. This is a commonly held view amongst stakeholders in both feminist organisations and the childcare sector more generally. The nature of this 'fragmented system' is one that leads parents having to 'cobble together' their arrangements in order to have their children properly looked after. Indeed, 40 per cent of local authorities in Scotland reported 'large gaps in provision' in 2013, with the problem being most acute for parents who have '"atypical" work patterns' (Family and Childcare Trust 2014: 18).

The cost of childcare is very high in Scotland. According to the Family and Childcare Trust's (2014: 14) report on childcare in Scotland, the average family can expect to pay £7,397 a year on childcare, which is 22 per cent higher than the average annual mortgage repayment (£6,053). The overlapping obstacles of patchy provision and high cost mean that, for some women, it is sometimes better to not go back to work or take up poorly-paid part-time employment instead. This perpetuates inequality between men and women. Because women tend to have lower wages, it is their income that is often dispensable when difficult choices have to be made. Both the costs and the lack of provision, particularly in rural areas, mean that women quite often leave work and then find it difficult to get back into senior roles that they may well have held before having children.

The example of Sweden is again relevant here. The Swedish Government decided to invest in an extensive publicly financed childcare programme in the mid-1970s, driven partly by a desire to create a more gender-equal society. Since many mothers with pre-school children were already in the labour market, demand for childcare far exceeded supply. In order to meet demand, a legal guarantee was given in 1985 that all children between the ages of eighteen months and five years would receive a childcare place by 1991. Demand continued to exceed supply, however, and so legislation passed in 1995 meant that municipalities were required to provide a childcare place within three to four months. There is therefore near universal childcare provision in Sweden, and municipalities quite often offer childcare during evenings, weekends and school holidays. The objective of gender equality has consistently been a driving force in these developments.

In Sweden, a maximum fee for parents was introduced in 2002 in order to increase childcare accessibility, but also to improve the economic circumstances of families with children and to facilitate mothers' participation in the workforce. The maximum fee means that a ceiling is set on the amount of money that a municipality (including the independent pre-schools) can charge parents. Households with an income of over SEK 42,000 (around £3,075) per month pay at most the maximum fee; other households pay at most a certain percentage of their gross income. The maximum fee was a voluntary scheme, but those municipalities that joined the system were entitled to a special central government grant to compensate them for the loss of income resulting from the reduction in fees paid by parents. The maximum fee had a very high take-up; only two municipalities out of a total of 290 decided to wait before introducing the reform in the first year. In 2000, parental fees in pre-school covered 15 per cent of the total cost, which fell to 8 per cent percent in 2013, largely as a result of the maximum fee. According to the OECD (2012), childcare costs averaged 4.7 per cent of total family income.

Getting mothers into work through a better childcare system is one thing, but the quality of employment also matters. Low wages, part-time hours and zero-hours contracts are just some of the issues regarding the types of jobs that many women, particularly those who are experiencing poverty themselves, can expect to face. The UK Government's welfare reforms are believed to be making this situation worse. So, although there is the issue of childcare provision which needs to be addressed, the problem is a far deeper one, and is rooted in the UK's approach to social security and the current economic model. Recent research presented to the UK Parliament has indeed suggested that gaining employment is no guarantee of escaping poverty (UK Government 2013).

Childcare is not enough – the importance of parental leave

Cultural context is crucially important in understanding not only how gender equal a particular society is, but how effective policies designed to make a society more gender equal will be (Budig, Misra and Boeckmann 2009; Keck and Saraceno 2013). Childcare is a crucial piece of this policy jigsaw, but the societies that are the most gender equal usually have an overall approach to family policy that is conducive to encouraging gender equality. In order to promote a society that encourages more men into the care domain as well as supporting women into employment (Pascall and Lewis 2004), a coherent family policy which includes a parental scheme that incorporates fathers in a fundamental way is essential (Van Lancker and Ghysels 2013). Parental leave schemes can encourage fathers to share leave from the workplace and therefore take a more active role in childcare. Alternatively, a different parental leave approach can strengthen gender roles by encouraging mothers to stay at home and abandon the public sphere.

In Iceland, there is broad political and societal support for mixed leave policies and, as a result, there is a high take-up of paternity leave. In 2007, for example, 88.5 per cent of fathers took up shared leave, and Icelandic fathers take more paternity days compared to the other Nordic countries (Bjork-Eydal 2012: 42–4). In Denmark, the allocation of paternal leave was scaled back, which had a subsequent and negative knock-on effect on gender equality (Haas and Rostgaard 2011). Despite this gap, Saxonberg (2013: 36) identifies Sweden and Norway, as well as Iceland, as good proponents of degenderising family policies, with Germany also improving, although its childcare policies are still genderising compared to degenderising parental leave policies (Saxonberg 2013: 44).

Research into Norwegian parental leave suggests that fathers' leave quota is seen almost as a 'gift' that fathers feel they cannot turn down (Brandth and Kvande 2012: 63). Furthermore, shared parental leave is more likely when couples both have high-status jobs – so this relative equality in wages means a more contracted negotiation takes place between parents (Brandth and Kvande 2012: 65). Evidence from Australia suggests that when 'carer-friendly flexibility' is offered to parents, men have a much lower take-up of such schemes because they are not offered on a 'take-it-or-leave-it' basis (Charlesworth 2013: 377). Indeed, both a carrot and a stick approach is required: the salary remuneration needs to be generous enough to mean that fathers do not take too heavy a drop in income and thus elect not to take the leave, but also a 'take-it-or-leave it' approach is required whereby leave cannot be transferred to the mother; if the father does not take up the minimum allocation then it is lost.

As it stands, the Scottish Parliament has little to no jurisdiction over parental leave policy. Therefore, any policy agenda which seeks to promote gender equality and which contains a childcare policy strategy will be incomplete and will, in the long run, have a limited effect. That said, this is based on the assumption that the policy direction taken by the UK Government will not be conducive to the encouragement of gender equality in Scotland. Indeed, the UK Government has legislated for the creation of a shared parental leave scheme, but it remains to be seen if this policy has any long-term impact. In order to promote gender equality in Scotland and move towards a system in the mould of Sweden or Iceland, parental leave policy needs to be aligned with childcare policy in an overarching gender equality strategy. Therefore, for gender equality advocates, the devolution of powers over parental leave would be a logical step to take.

The independence referendum and the resulting No vote

In the run-up to the referendum on Scottish independence, the Scottish Government published a White Paper, *Scotland's Future*, which provided a blueprint of what an independent Scotland would look like. The document made explicit a commitment to depart from the UK Government's social security policies post-2008, recognising that this affected particular groups (including women living in poverty) and believing that 'it is possible to design an efficient and fair welfare system that meets the needs of those who depend on it, and treats them with dignity and respect while supporting those who can into work' (Scottish Government 2013: 154–5).

In order to achieve the economic and social changes it envisaged in an independent Scotland, the Scottish Government placed childcare at the centre of its proposals for an independent Scotland, presenting it in social investment terms:

> Extensive provision of early learning and childcare for all families is a hallmark of some of the most advanced and successful countries today. There is a wide range of evidence indicating the potential benefits of high quality, funded early learning and childcare, with all social groups benefiting from high quality pre-school provision and children from the poorest families gaining most from universal provision. (Scottish Government 2013: 192)

The mechanism for achieving this was through the provision of a guaranteed right to childcare provision for all over 2-year-olds. This was intended to tackle the fact that Scottish parents spend far more of their household income on childcare as compared to the average in OECD countries, thus making work uneconomic for many low-paid women. It also reflected the fact that investment in childcare leads to better outcomes for children and for working parents, addresses child poverty and leads to improved educational attainment.

This explicit linking of childcare to the independence referendum attracted criticism from two main sources. Pro-union parties pointed out that the Scottish Government already controlled many of the levers necessary to provide childcare, particularly through education and early years interventions.

Education policy was an explicitly devolved matter, as was control over the healthcare and social care budget. Feminists also pointed out that explicitly tying childcare to the ability to control the entire budget – and specifically linking a disinvestment in nuclear weapons to the provision of childcare – was aimed more at securing the votes of women and the anti-nuclear lobby for independence rather than a genuine desire for gender equality through childcare provision (Azong 2015; Azong and Wilinska 2016).

As we now know, the Scottish electorate opted against voting for independence. Therefore, the full range of fiscal and social security levers which would have been open to the Scottish Government had the result been different are not available. This is not to say that reform of childcare with the aim of promoting gender equality is impossible, of course. The Scottish Government has full control over the type of childcare services it wishes to deliver and fund, but it lacks the capacity to alter the social security system in such a way that money that would otherwise be given to parents to pay childcare providers could be redirected into a supply-side arrangement.

Furthermore, it was unclear to what extent the benefits resulting from increasing the female workforce would accrue to the Scottish Parliament. After the independence referendum, the Smith Commission recommended that almost full responsibility of income tax generated in Scotland should be devolved. In early 2016, the UK and Scottish Governments agreed a fiscal framework that stipulates the formula that will determine the level of the block grant that will accrue to Scotland. Therefore, there is now a clear incentive for the Scottish Government to try and increase income tax receipts and foster economic growth through opening up more opportunities for employment.

All of this is not an issue for gender equality in and of itself given that it is not impossible that a future UK Government could initiate a range of reforms that facilitated gender equality within the context of the powers it reserves. For example, legislation on shared parental leave came into effect in April 2015. The policy does not contain the 'stick' element which is essential for a truly transformational effect that was seen in Iceland. It nevertheless sets the basis upon which future reforms could be enacted and, on a societal level, signals to fathers that it is possible and indeed normal to take up a more extensive caring role with young children. In sum, social policy devolved in Scotland, such as childcare, could, in theory, be a key element in a UK-wide drive towards closing the gender gap. However, history tells us that this is unlikely, especially considering the current Conservative UK Government. Implementing policies that are conducive to gender equality at the devolved level may well be counteracted, even undone, by decisions taken by the UK Government.

What should Scotland do?

There are constraints on Scotland's capacity to develop a child-care system entirely of its own design given its constitutional relationship to the UK. It is also limited in how vociferously it can pursue a policy programme that promotes gender equality given the policy areas that are reserved. Under the Scotland Act (2016), there are now new options open to the Scottish Government (although many of those being considered were possible before further devolution). The first would be extending the amount of free childcare hours available for children from the age of three. These normally occur in a nursery setting and are available until the children go to school. Currently, these hours equate to just over three hours a day, a paltry amount for mothers who wish to work full time, or even part time. These hours should be at least doubled in order to cover more of the working day. Furthermore, most parents would not object to paying fees to contribute to extending such arrange-ments, provided that those fees were reasonable and mean that mothers would benefit financially from working longer hours. Such arrangements need to be in one setting so that parents do not have to organise informal childcare arrangements that may be susceptible to interruption.

The Scottish Government could also investigate how a supply-side model of funding can be created in Scotland. The difficulty is that the UK social security system works by paying parents money through the tax credits system to go towards paying their childcare costs. Therefore, moving towards a supply-side system while this remains in place means that features of a demand-side and a supply-side system would be in operation alongside one another, a situation that could create substantial confusion and inefficiencies. It is difficult to foresee how this situation could be resolved, although one potential solution could be that the childcare element of tax credits goes straight to the Scottish Parliament's budget as a ring-fenced source of funding that is then directed towards the provision of public childcare. However, this is almost certainly beyond the powers in the Scotland Act (2016).

The third policy area that the Scottish Government could look towards is parental leave. This is currently a reserved policy matter and there is very little chance of this becoming a devolved policy area at this current time. However, there is the potential for the Scottish Government to lobby the UK Government for more administrative control of parental leave, so that Scottish parental leave contained a 'stick' approach to fathers taking leave in the sense that parents would lose their entitlement to a particular amount if the father did not take it up. This is a complicated matter because it involves issues around income remuneration but there has already been a precedent set by the proposed devolution of the administration of Universal Credit.

The cases of Germany and Canada, however, show that there is scope for policy differentiation within federal systems. The Canadian Childcare Advocacy Association of Canada (CCAAC) always possessed a federalised structure to reflect its desire for a pan-Canadian approach. The centre has advocated childcare initiatives but has managed to articulate these preferences in a fairly ineffective fashion only. This is because it requires provinces to report progress in priority areas in a way which meant that there were limited means to hold failing provinces to account (Mahon and Collier 2010: 57). Handing over money to provinces to spend on childcare, the Conservative federal government of Stephen Harper did little to address the accountability problem in that it adhered strictly to the separation of powers as constituted in Canada (Mahon and Collier 2010: 58). Indeed, policy areas crucial to women's equality were put into the hands of provincial governments that lack fiscal clout and thus promote weak policy and find it difficult to step outside the confines of federal-provincial politics (Grace 2011: 101).

Within Canada, however, the case of Quebec stands out. In Quebec, childcare is a 'national' issue, linked to its nation-building project (Mahon and Collier 2010: 51). The Parti Québécois has traditionally had leading feminists within its ranks, and Quebec's prominent public service has also had effective femocrats in its ranks (Mahon and Collier 2010: 61), and there is coordinated childcare lobbying inside provincial family policy frames. Family policy has traditionally been designed partly to encourage higher birth rates and offers highly subsidised and universal child-care (Kottelenberg and Lehrer 2013: 265). In 1997, a childcare programme at CAN$5 per day was launched and gradually extended to pre- and after-school and to all children. By 2011, over half of the children in Quebec were in regulated day care, compared with one-fifth elsewhere in Canada (Fortin, Godbout and St-Cerny 2012). Quebec has a higher proportion of women participating in work compared to the rest of Canada (Beaujot, Du and Ravanera 2013), and its childcare policy has led to a decrease in families with the most 'complete' division in labour and a reduced effect of education and age on parents' strategies when it comes to balancing employment and care (Stalker and Ornstein 2013: 258). It has been calculated that there is a net fiscal gain – with the taxes paid by new women workers exceeding the cost of the programme – but that this is unevenly distributed since the Quebec Government meets the entire bill while the federal government gets more of the tax benefit (Fortin, Godbout and St-Cerny 2012).

Quebec has also introduced more generous parental leave provisions under its Labour Standards Act. In 2006 it provided for more paid leave, including an element for fathers which cannot be transferred to the mother. These are financed from Quebec's share of the federal programme that provides the basic cover elsewhere under the national employment insurance scheme, together with additional contributions from employers and employees.

In Germany, federal legislation was passed in 2008 which stipulated a legal right to public childcare, either within an institutional setting or by a childminder. This legislation became operational in 2013, with the German Government proposing coverage for one-third of all under-3's by 2013. Despite policy developments in Germany facilitating gender equality, individual states still have a lot of flexibility around how they administrate crucial policy areas such as parental leave. For example, Bavaria has been in a position to administer parental leave in such a way that it undermines policy direction from the centre and continues to support the male-breadwinner model (MacRae 2010). Therefore, the realities of multilevel governance and the politics of different territories can have a profound impact on policy outcomes.

Such policy changes would create some important conditions for Scotland becoming a more gender-equal country. The example of Quebec shows that significant policy divergence in this area is possible and does indeed work. Obviously, any developments in the Scottish context must navigate the constitutional context particular to Scotland, but developments towards further devolution of social security policy have been set by the Smith Commission and so a willing Scottish Government can aspire to gather more powers from the UK Government in order to make such a project a reality.

Conclusion

Now that income tax receipts are to be devolved to Scotland in their entirety, there is a greater incentive than ever for the Scottish Government to grow the economy and, as a result, increase the amount of revenues generated from income tax. One way of doing this would be to increase childcare provision and thus allow for higher levels of maternal employment, which in turn would increase economic activity. Simply putting more and better childcare provision in place would encourage this, but if the overall aim of the Scottish Government is to make Scotland a more gender-equal country then more would need to be done to bring fathers further into the caring sphere while, simultaneously, encouraging more mothers into the employment sphere. A concerted, feminist-led pressure is required for this to happen and it remains to be seen if that pressure is strong enough in the Scottish context in the way that it was in the case of Quebec or in Sweden.

This chapter has shown that the best practice on childcare policy means supply-side funding, universal coverage, low fees and wraparound care. Furthermore, parental leave is a key policy issue that facilitates gender equality in that it brings fathers into the care sphere while simultaneously supporting mothers in the job market. Scotland is able to legislate for most of these issues, but the social security system remains a reserved issue. Therefore, it is not within the gift of the Scottish Government to push for an all-encompassing childcare strategy that can truly promote a more gender-equal society.

There is always the possibility that social security could become fully devolved. The Smith Commission recommended that some administrative aspects of the Universal Credit system be devolved to Scotland. This was duly contained within the Scotland Act (2016) but it remains to be seen what impact this has on social security in Scotland. However, a precedent has been set for the devolution of social security that may well have a bearing on future constitutional negotiations and restructuring. It will be up to feminist campaigners, therefore, both within and outside political parties, to push for the devolution of policy areas like parental leave.

Nevertheless, the literature shows that institutions and policies are not enough. Societal and cultural congeniality is required for any project that aims to make the economy and society more gender equal. Feminists know this more than most and realise that a gender-equal society may take a generation to come about because sexism is a deeply engrained phenomenon. This is not to say that policy and institutional and constitutional structures do not matter, but it would likely take a decade at least before the impact of any such policies on, or any real change in, gender relations could be identified.

6 Constitutional Change, Social Investment and Prevention Policy in Scotland

Paul Cairney, Malcolm Harvey and Emily St Denny

Introduction

Constitutional change provides an opportunity to debate radical policy change. In Scotland, the prospect of independence or the devolution of significantly new powers allowed its advocates and political commentators the chance to reconsider the Scottish Government's policy choices and the way in which it makes and delivers policy. Issues of social policy, social justice and how to organise public spending during a long period of 'austerity' became central to political debate in the years leading up to the referendum (Mooney and Scott 2015).

While the idea of social investment had been popular for some time, it grew in importance during the constitutional debate. It fits well with the vague idea – promoted by many organisations, including the SNP – that Scottish independence is a social democratic project, offering an alternative to austerity politics and neo-liberalism. It also complements an existing Scottish Government agenda to reduce inequalities and address its decreasing budget by reducing acute public service demand through early intervention and prevention policies.

Social investment and prevention are closely related concepts with major implications for policy and policy making in Scotland. Both highlight the value of investment in human capital (Chapter 1), and are linked closely to the Scottish Government's preferred method of governance – the Scottish Approach to Policymaking – associated with terms such as social partnership, co-production and assets based approaches (Cairney, Russell and St Denny 2016).

However, we draw on two public policy concepts to show that, although the referendum provided this opportunity for public debate, we should not exaggerate its impact on government policy. The first concept is ambiguity: broad policy aims lack meaning unless they are operationalised in detail. This process was often absent during the referendum debate. Instead, groups with little chance of policy influence made broad and often heroic claims of radical policy change to come, while the Scottish Government was more modest or vague in its intentions. It is easier to identify buzz words or slogans for policy reform and broad long-term aspirations than specific aims and objectives, and therefore it is difficult to tell if those objectives would compete with the day-to-day business of government. Social investment is rarely properly defined, and prevention often describes a philosophy of government or broad aspiration rather than a specific policy agenda delivered in practice.

Second, we draw on Kingdon's (1984) multiple streams analysis (MSA) to identify the difference between a window of opportunity to *recommend* and *deliver* reforms. MSA suggests that major policy change occurs during a brief window of opportunity when: attention to a problem is high; a well-thought-out solution exists; and policy makers have the motive and opportunity to adopt it. These three streams are not sequential. Rather, they represent three necessary but insufficient conditions for major policy change. We argue that, although reformers were optimistic about these streams coming together to produce major policy change during the window provided by constitutional change, they were likely to be disappointed. With social investment and prevention, policy makers are pursuing a vague solution to an unclear problem and have yet to work out how to deliver their aims. Further, although Scottish independence could have made a difference, we caution against assuming that major constitutional change produces policy change, by showing that (a) many obstacles to reforms are related generally to policy making rather than specifically to Scotland, and (b) the pressures to reform are often prompted more by other factors such as budgetary constraint.

However, there are some signs that Scottish politics and government can produce important changes in these areas. So, in the final sections, we discuss how key actors can take forward the agenda on social investment, and how the Scottish Government is currently making sense of prevention as part of its attempts to produce evidence-based policy. With social investment, we discuss the extent to which the Scottish Government can learn from international experience, such as when exploring a 'Nordic' approach. With prevention, we show that it is drawing lessons from several potentially successful approaches to policy change.

Policy ambiguity: how do actors make sense of social investment and prevention policy in Scotland?

Broadly speaking, social investment and prevention are similar and complementary terms used to reframe public service delivery as an investment in human capital. They can also involve similar objectives, such as to reduce socioeconomic inequalities and the demand for public services. Social investment, according to Keating (Chapter 1), is used to reframe certain forms of public service expenditure in infrastructure, and services such as education as a potential contribution to, rather than inevitable drain on, the economy. Prevention involves a similar sense of capital investment for the long term, but it can refer to range of policies, from those intended to deliver the savings and benefits that result from intervening as early as possible in people's lives to improve their life chances, to the prevention of falls in older people (Cairney, Russell and St Denny 2016). So, the loose usage of such terms in public debate might produce the sense that they are synonymous but, in fact, they merely overlap significantly in key areas. Social investment is the term used more frequently during the referendum, while prevention has a recent history in Scottish Government strategy, primarily from 2011.

The referendum as a platform for social investment

The referendum gave advocacy groups an unusually large platform on which to articulate radical socioeconomic policy reforms. Most notably, the Common Weal (2016) project provided the strongest commitment to the social investment model. It drew in particular on Nordic experiences to produce guiding principles to 'achieve a Scotland of social and economic equality'. Proposals with Nordic influences include: a more progressive taxation system; a welfare system based on active labour market policies; nationalisation of public transport systems; and a commitment to universalism as a means to foster social solidarity. More importantly, the referendum provided the SNP (as the party leading the Scottish Government) with the opportunity to outline its vision of an independent Scotland. Its White Paper *Scotland's Future* (Scottish Government 2013) advocated the social investment strategy of Nordic states. First, it framed government spending on public services, including education, research, healthcare and childcare, as investment in measures to improve economic and social conditions. For example, investment in childcare and early years education could increase the number of working mothers and improve attainment levels:

> ensuring that there is high-quality readily available childcare supports parents to find sustained employment, but it is also an investment in children to give them the best start in life. And, as a result of this early investment, when those children go on to achieve their full potential, they will repay that investment through their productivity and creativity as active members of a more cohesive society. (Scottish Government 2013: 161)

Second, redefining public spending as investment and social spending established a clearer link between unemployment benefits, training and preparation for employment, emphasising that welfare payments should be seen not as a government handout but as an investment in that citizen's future employability. The aim was to balance economic competitiveness (and employability) with improvements to social conditions:

> a social investment approach starts from the premise that the delivery of welfare services should not be seen as simply a safety net for individuals who cannot support themselves. Instead they should be seen as an opportunity for positive investment in people throughout their lives. (Scottish Government 2013: 160)

The explicit argument of *Scotland's Future* was that small states are better equipped to deliver the infrastructure and harness the societal attitudes required for a social investment approach (Scottish Government 2013: 160). In turn, social investment would reinforce:

> a culture in society that is more inclusive, more respectful and more equal. It also places the cash transfers that people traditionally think of as welfare – such as out of work benefits and tax credits – in

a wider, more cost-effective and socially beneficial context when
viewed over the longer-term. (Scottish Government 2013: 162)

It refers to shared responsibility and a social partnership between
the government and citizens, using Nordic experiences to demonstrate how social investment could reduce unemployment,
increase earnings *and* grow economies (Scottish Government
2013: 161).

The Scottish Government articulated these plans in the
context of a debate on the adequacy of devolution or further
devolution. It tended to describe a sense of stymied progress
under devolution; that it was doing its best to make major
reforms, but that its plans could only go so far. A key example
is childcare, because it could (a) argue that it had the powers
to invest but not to recoup the economic benefits of the investment, and (b) provide a way to partially operationalise social
investment, combining specific short-term plans with broader
and longer-term aims and predictions (see Chapter 5).

So, on the one hand, it could describe plans that would
largely be rolled out regardless of the referendum result –
increasing childcare initially by allocating 600 hours per year
for three- and four-year-olds (and vulnerable two-year-olds)
during the 2016–21 parliamentary session, and promising to
expand further under independence to 1,140 hours (Scottish
Government 2013: 194–5). It could also describe the long-term
benefits to parents and children, capital investment in facili-
ties, new jobs in childcare services, and the chance for 100,000
parents (predominantly mothers) to return to the workforce. Its
argument was that enabling more women to return to the workforce allowed the policy to pay for itself, and that the provision
of childcare services is part of a broader package of policies
around employment, welfare and economic growth (Scottish
Government 2013: 194–5).

The Scottish Government took a similar approach with prevention, although its policy strategy in this field was better
established and *Scotland's Future* simply proposed to extend
the so-called Scottish Approach to Policymaking (Cairney,
Russell and St Denny 2016) by 'joining together those services that are currently under UK control with those currently
delivered by Scottish organizations' (Scottish Government
2013: 359). The Scottish Parliament Finance Committee (2011)
and Scottish Government both saw prevention as a way to

reduce socioeconomic inequalities and the costs of public services driven by unnecessary demand. The latter commissioned the Christie Commission to examine these issues in November 2010 (Commission of the Future Delivery of Public Services 2011). The Commission prompted the Scottish Government to address its unintended contribution to a cycle of deprivation and low aspiration by redirecting spending, encouraging public bodies to have shared budgets and aims, and engaging 'communities' in the design of public services – as part of an assets-based approach (Commission of the Future Delivery of Public Services 2011: 27).

The Scottish Government's (2011b: 6) response was positive, signalling 'a decisive shift towards prevention' and 'a holistic approach to addressing inequalities'. It sought to turn this broad agenda into specific aims and projects by listing its existing prevention-led projects, announcing three new funds (£500 million) and outlining specific priorities, such as the expansion of childcare, up to 2016.

Yet, this was a decisive shift towards a vague policy solution. The meaning of prevention, and related terms such as early intervention, is not clear. We can describe with some certainty the ends described by governments, such as to reduce inequalities and public service costs by addressing the root causes of inequality and service demand. We can also identify the types of long-standing problems that they seek to address, including crime and anti-social behaviour, ill health and unhealthy behaviour, low educational attainment, unemployment and low employability, as well as newer problems relating to climate change and anti-environmental behaviour. However, we can be less sure about the means, beyond the desire to shift from a focus on poverty and redistribution towards reintegrating individuals 'into society and allowing them to make their contribution to economic and social life' (Keating 2010: 243).

Prevention can be linked closely to the idea of early intervention, and the terms may often be used interchangeably, but they are not synonymous. Early intervention is often used to focus on young children, to describe pre-school or parenting programmes. Prevention often refers to a broader age range; it includes strategies for older people. Both may be related to a notional spectrum, from successful prevention/early intervention to stop problems arising, to an attempt to stop more harm occurring:

1. *Primary prevention* – stop a problem occurring by investing early and/or modifying the social or physical environment. Focus on the whole population.
2. *Secondary prevention* – identify a problem at a very early stage to minimize harm. Identify and focus on at-risk groups.
3. *Tertiary prevention* – stop a problem getting worse. Identify and focus on affected groups. (Gough 2013: 3)

Consequently, 'prevention' is vague enough to describe almost all government activity. Therefore, unless governments make a specific commitment to primary or secondary prevention, the ambiguity may allow them to make a commitment to prevention policies which are often similar to reactive policies dealing with current problems. Or, a vague reference to prevention allows service providers to rebrand their activities as preventive without shifting their approach.

Overall, social investment, prevention and early intervention are terms which describe broad philosophies of government without specific objectives. The Scottish Government has begun to operationalise key aspects, such as in its childcare strategy, but without providing a way to demonstrate progress towards its aims.

Has there been a window of opportunity for policy change?

Kingdon (1984) famously challenged the value of the phrase 'an idea whose time has come' to describe the introduction of significant new policies. An idea's time may come only when certain conditions are met. The phrase 'window of opportunity' suggests that heightened levels of attention are fleeting; that people only have a short time in which to produce a policy solution, and persuade policy makers to select it, before their attention lurches elsewhere. Successfully exploiting a window of opportunity is not inevitable, and the opportunity to produce major change is rare.

Subsequent 'multiple streams' studies produced the insight that problems do not receive attention simply because we think they are important, and policy makers do not select solutions simply because they are the most effective (Cairney and Jones 2016; Jones et al. 2016).

This is not a comprehensively rational process in which, in this order: elected policy makers articulate their values, rank their aims and prioritise which problems to solve; government bureaucracies gather all the information necessary to produce solutions; and policy makers select the best solutions. Rather, Kingdon draws on Cohen, March and Olsen's (1972) 'garbage can' model of policy making in organisations, which suggests that policy-makers' aims and policy problems are ambiguous and bureaucrats struggle to research issues and produce viable solutions quickly. Sometimes people wait for the right time to present their ready-made solutions. Sometimes aimless policy makers just want to look busy and decisive. So, problem identification, solution production and choice are separate processes, each of which is a necessary but insufficient condition for major policy change. They are described in MSA as three separate 'streams' which must come together at the same time.

1. *Problem stream – attention lurches to a policy problem.* Problems are policy issues which are deemed to require attention. There are no objective indicators to determine which problems deserve attention, and perceptions of problems can change quickly. Problems get attention based on how they are framed or defined by participants who compete for attention – using evidence to address uncertainty and persuasion to address ambiguity. In some cases, issues receive attention because of a crisis or change in the scale of the problem. Only a tiny fraction of problems receive policy-maker attention. Getting attention is a major achievement which must be acted upon quickly, before attention shifts elsewhere. This might be achieved by demonstrating that a well thought out solution already exists.

2. *Policy stream – a solution to that problem is available.* While attention lurches quickly from issue to issue, viable solutions involving major policy change take time to develop. Kingdon (1984: 130–1) describes ideas in a 'policy primeval soup', evolving as they are proposed by one actor then reconsidered and modified by a large number of participants, who may have to be softened up to new ideas. To deal with the disconnect between lurching attention and slow policy development, they develop widely-accepted solutions in anticipation of future problems, then find the right time to exploit or encourage attention to a relevant problem.

3. *Politics stream – policy makers have the motive and oppor-tunity to turn this solution into policy.* They have to pay attention to the problem and be receptive to the proposed solution. They may supplement their own beliefs with their perception of the national mood and the feedback they receive from interest groups and political parties. In some cases, only a change of government may be enough to provide that motive.

Overall, the metaphors of separate streams and a window of opportunity suggest that policy change requires a degree of, if not serendipity, at least a confluence of events and actions in a short space of time. Successful advocates of change know that a policy solution generally has to go through a 'process of consideration, floating up, discussion, revision and trying out again' before it will be selected and, therefore, 'advocates lie in wait in and around government with their solutions at hand, waiting for problems to float by to which they can attach their solutions, waiting for a development in the political stream they can use to their advantage' (Kingdon 1984: 149, 165–6). The emphasis is on a need to explain, often in some depth, why that opportunity may arise only at a particular time and place, and/ or why there are so many missed opportunities when attention to a problem fades before a feasible solution can be produced.

The window of opportunity for social investment and prevention

We can use MSA to provide a contrast between the hopes for social investment and prevention, described by advocacy groups and the Scottish Government, and the actual results so far. We argue that many advocates treat social investment and prevention as ideas whose times have come. In other words, they think that the Scottish Government has produced policy during a window of opportunity, paying high attention to the problems of high inequalities and public service costs; produc-ing detailed and feasible solutions to each problem; and display-ing the motive and opportunity to select human capital-style solutions. Yet, the actual development of policy suggests that they paid attention to an ill-defined problem and produced a solution which often proves to be too vague to operationalise in a simple way. Prevention and social investment could represent ideas whose time comes and goes without producing the concrete policy changes that their supporters expected.

The experience of social investment and prevention, so far, suggests that the detailed aims of advocates and governments are difficult to pin down. The problem stream seems unclear since a series of problems may come together at the same time to produce a demand for these policies. Indeed, prevention has, for some time, generated widespread but superficial consensus, bringing together groups on the left, seeking to reduce poverty and inequality, as well as groups on the right, seeking to reduce economic inactivity and the costs of public services (Billis 1981: 367). On each occasion on which attention rises to prevention, there is great temptation to treat it as a cure to several related problems: an era of austerity in which governments face the need to reduce budgets and deliver a comparable public service at lower cost; the need to reduce demand for acute public services by addressing socioeconomic problems at an early stage; and a desire to reduce the kinds of inequalities (related, for example, to income) associated with social problems. As such, its attractiveness is clear and, in the UK, it has been a theme pursued in official reports, during Labour and Conservative governments, since the 1950s (Billis 1981: 368). However, this abstract appeal masks the need to make specific and hard choices, such as between universal services, which may foster solidarity but also benefit the middle classes disproportionately, and targetted interventions, which may foster greater stigma but benefit target populations. When the mask slips, cross-party cooperation and government enthusiasm dips.

Furthermore, prevention's policy stream has unusual features that illustrate some of the universal challenges to policy making (Cairney, Russell and St Denny 2016). Its source of attractiveness to policy makers may also be its main flaw: it is possible to adopt prevention as a broad idea without knowing how to turn it into a series of concrete objectives. Indeed, a focus on prevention reminds us that the word 'idea' means at least two things: a specific policy solution to a clearly defined problem, or a potentially useful but vague way of thinking about a complex and perhaps intractable (wicked) problem. In the case of the latter, the window of opportunity may not produce the sort of policy change that policy makers expect. Instead, we may see a groundswell of attention to, and support for, a policy solution that is very difficult to operationalise. We may find that everyone agrees on the broad solution, but no one agrees on the detail, causing governments to spend years making very little progress.

A focus on superficial learning from other countries complicates this process further. While actors such as the Scottish Government expressed the desire to pursue 'Nordic' social investment, it did so in the absence of a single and well-defined Nordic model (Keating and Harvey 2014; Harvey 2015). Rather, the Common Weal and *Scotland's Future* used romanticised notions of Nordic policy making, drawing upon (often contradictory) elements and philosophies apparent in different Nordic states. Further, their proposals rarely included reference to the key institutional elements – absent or underdeveloped in Scotland – that allowed those states to develop social investment systems. In particular, Scotland lacks the tripartite bargaining between governments, employers and unions that has long been associated with Nordic systems (even though, for example, such arrangements no longer exist in Sweden – Cairney and Widfeldt 2015).

The politics stream is also complicated by the close link between policy as a set of policy instruments and governance principles, or a set of ideas about the way in which they should be administered and delivered. In both cases (but prevention in particular), policy is linked almost inextricably to the Scottish Approach to Policymaking (Cairney 2015; Cairney, Russell and St Denny 2016) which involves a commitment to:

- pursue joined-up or holistic government, to foster cooperation between, and secure a common aim for, departments, public bodies and stakeholders at several levels of government – or at least to coordinate a range of government objectives to address problems that cut across traditional departments;
- redefine the role of central government by encouraging (a) localism, or fostering the capacity of local communities to tailor national policies to their areas, and/or (b) the sharing of policy-making responsibility across the public sector and in partnership with non-governmental bodies;
- tailor public services to their users, encouraging a focus on the assets of individuals, and inviting users to participate and co-produce their services;

- move away from unhelpful short-term targets (as proxies for policy aims) and performance management, which produce major unintended consequences, towards more meaningful and long-term outcomes-based measures of policy success and population well-being;
- rely extensively on evidence-based policy making to identify which projects produce the most benefit and deserve investment.

These principles are also apparent in the UK Government's prevention agenda, but the Scottish Government has sought to articulate a Scottish model (Elvidge 2011) or Scottish 'approach' (Housden 2014), which is allegedly more consultative and participatory, and less centralist, than its UK comparator. Consequently, Scottish ministers may select prevention as a solution but devolve responsibility for policy delivery and outcomes to a large number, and wide range, of organisations in the public and private sector. Policy progress is particularly difficult to predict because prevention is a vague policy, many bodies have high discretion and many competing priorities, and the Scottish Government is relatively content to 'let go' rather than micro-manage.

What would it take to turn these broad aims into specific policies and outcomes?

Adapting meaningful lessons from international experience of social investment would be one solution to the problems we describe. For example, a shift to a full-scale Nordic-style social investment model would require several components – some of which were identified in *Scotland's Future*, while others were not. The ideal-typical Nordic model, most closely followed by Norway, combines a comprehensive social security system with institutionalised social rights, social solidarity, and a tripartite bargaining system that requires cooperation between employers' associations, employees (organised through widespread unionisation) and the government (Brandal, Bratberg and Thorsen 2013). It requires high levels of taxation to provide for generous active labour market policies such as universal unemployment and sickness insurance, and correspondingly high levels of employment to ensure that revenue from taxation exceeds spending on welfare payments. It requires high levels of social solidarity, which might be achieved through universal programmes (for example, by ensuring that the middle classes receive the benefits they pay for through taxation).

Scotland currently lacks many of these components of the Norwegian social investment model. First, neither Scotland nor the wider UK have the tripartite bargaining system which proved so central to industrial relations and wage bargaining in Norway and which allows for a reconciliation of individual wages and the social wage (see Chapter 2). The UK toyed with corporatism in the 1960s and 1970s, and though it played a successful role in limiting wage and price increases during periods of inflation, the system broke down in the early 1980s, amid hostility from the Thatcher Government and soured relations with trade unions. Weakness on all three sides (militant grass-roots trade unions, weak organisation on the part of business, and a government disinclined to compromise in the wake of strikes) led to the failure of corporatism in the UK (Keating and Harvey 2014). In the thirty years since, there has been limited formal space where relations between business, trade unions and government could be resurrected, and agreements have been limited.

Second, Scotland within the UK lacks the same sense of social solidarity driven by universalism. While the social investment model in Norway provides social services – unemployment insurance, healthcare, childcare and education – on a universal basis, welfare provision in the UK is more selective.

Third, the Scottish Parliament/Government does not have the full power over taxation and social security to make explicit links between taxing and spending to support social investment, or to combine (for example) high levels of income and land taxes with those (such as on consumption) which are more regressive but less susceptible to avoidance schemes (Bell and Eiser 2014a).

Fourth, there is great potential for inconsistent UK/Scottish strategies: for the Scottish Government to oversee a spending regime that favours the wealthy and middle classes on universal free services with no means testing, while the UK Government maintains a tax and benefits policy that many people will perceive to be insufficiently redistributive. The Scottish Government has also signalled a commitment to reduce or maintain the levels of the taxes it controls.

Finally, future tax and spending commitments remain under-debated. *Scotland's Future* indicated that while the Scottish Government planned on substantive capital outlays on child-care and other social investments, it also planned to maintain levels of income and local taxation and reduce corporation taxes to encourage inward investment.

In that context, a major shift to social investment would have been possible in an independent Scotland, but built on two difficult steps. The first is extending its own brand of con-sultation and negotiation (the Scottish 'approach') to economic policies to develop a more corporatist style. This would build on its record of modest success in developing a tripartite rela-tionship between the Scottish Government, local authorities and teaching unions in education (Cairney 2013), as well as its ability to negotiate with unions in a more conciliatory way in health.

The second is linking taxing and spending closely, to justify taxation increases by reframing them as part of investments in public services and social security, and to make sure that most people believe that universalism is in their collective interest (Rothstein 2001). A sense of a honeymoon period of constitutional change and political reform may have provided a window of opportunity for such changes. In the absence of independence, this shift to social investment seems more difficult but not impossible. The Scottish Government has formed 'territorial policy communities' (Keating, Cairney and Hepburn 2009) and generally enjoys good relationships with interest, voluntary, professional, and business groups, but based largely on the delivery of public services. It now has greater taxation and spending powers, but they do not allow the Scottish Government to make fundamental shifts in policy. There appears to be little demand in Scotland for an increase in taxation, or indeed any variation in taxation between what is paid in Scotland and what is paid in the rest of the UK (Harvey 2015), and there is no major event to prompt a temporary shift in attitudes. We may therefore see the continuation of a more pragmatic approach to social solidarity, to keep the middle classes happy with free and universal services while trying to find ways to target interventions to reduce inequalities (Cairney 2016a).

Overcoming 'universal' problems with prevention policies

Another potential solution is to address the problems that all governments face when they try to reduce ambiguity by specifying their aims in sufficient detail. The likely problems include: their commitment can diminish when they better understand the scale of the task; they have an electoral incentive to address more pressing issues of acute service delivery; their performance management systems are still geared towards short-term targets and outputs; they are wary of redistributive measures to reduce societal inequalities, and of measures to limit individual liberties; and they can only draw on very limited evidence of policy success (Cairney and St Denny 2015). Governments also face complexity: outcomes and actions emerge from complex policy-making systems, often despite central government attempts at control.

Scottish prevention policy seems to be based primarily on a pragmatic response to such problems of complexity: governments accept their limitations and delegate more decisions on policy implementation and service delivery to local actors. Yet they face a continuous trade-off between central and local control, and the unintended consequences of whatever balance they attempt to strike. When they seek central control, they encounter limits to joined-up government at the centre and emergent outcomes beyond their control at local levels. When they encourage local discretion, and the involvement of users and communities in service delivery, they encounter problems of accountability when there does not seem to be a meaningful nationally-driven strategy, and there is high potential to identify a 'postcode lottery' in which people receive a different level of service according to where they live (Cairney, Russell and St Denny 2016: 2).

The latter problem highlights some unintended consequences: the Scottish Government initially makes policy nationally in concert with many groups, but then it provides minimal local direction or compulsion, producing the sense within such groups that their influence is limited unless they can repeat their success at local levels (Cairney 2009, 2011: 135, 2014: 10). This new requirement for multiple lobbying strategies produces new imbalances of influence and a counter-intuitive sense that participants may, to all intents and purposes, become disillusioned with this national style of consultation. In particular, groups with limited resources may be the least supportive of flexible delivery arrangements because they only have the ability to influence the initial Scottish Government choice. When national governments make policy commitments that lack detailed restrictions, and leave the final outcome to the organisations that deliver policy, these groups perceive their initial influence to diminish during implementation (Cairney 2009: 366).

This new form of Scottish policy making combines with a new financial reality which changes further the nature of consultation. The first eight years of devolution were marked by nationally-driven policy making and significant increases in public expenditure. There were comparatively few policy disagreements and departments or groups were competing for additional resources. Most services were well funded but they did not contribute substantially to a reduction in socioeconomic, health or educational inequalities. Now, central governments have become increasingly likely to delegate power and encourage local governments and their stakeholders to make a greater impact on inequalities, at a reduced cost. The further devolution of power, combined with the new economic climate, produces new tensions between national and local policy makers and interest groups.

A Scottish model of prevention and early intervention: pragmatism and experimentation with three approaches

The Scottish Government's response to these problems has been to experiment on a small scale with three main approaches to prevention (Cairney 2015). Each approach allows actors to make sense of prevention in particular areas, and to provide a different balance between centralisation and localism, driven largely by different approaches to 'evidence-based policymaking' (Housden 2014: 71; Cairney 2016b).

The first is the importation or spread of innovative projects using criteria associated with evidence-based medicine. With this approach, policies become highly regarded because there is empirical evidence that they have been successful elsewhere (usually in other countries). In health departments, this evidence tends to be gathered with reference to 'evidence-based medicine' (EBM), or the argument that there is a hierarchy of good evidence in which randomised control trials (RCTs) and their systematic review are at the top, while user feedback and professional experience are closer to the bottom. So, evidence of success comes from, for example, an RCT conducted multiple times under similar conditions in multiple places.

If accepted as the basis for public service delivery, this approach has major implications for local autonomy. The RCT demonstrates the success of a very specific intervention with a set dosage. Further, the interventions require fidelity, to ensure that the active ingredient is given in the correct dosage, and to measure the model's effectiveness. In such cases, the projects are relatively likely to be funded and controlled by central governments, and linked to an 'implementation science' agenda in which we consider how best to roll out – often *uniformly* – the most successful evidence-based interventions in as many areas as possible (Nilsen et al. 2013). The Family Nurse Partnership (FNP) is a key example (Cairney 2015).

The second is a storytelling approach based on the rejection of an evidential hierarchy and the need to 'scale up' projects uniformly. Practitioners make reference to principles of good practice, and the value of practitioner and service user testimony. With this approach, the evidence on applicability to local areas comes from service users and practitioners: they use stories, conversations and practice-based or user feedback measures of success to help us decide if a project is successful and worth adopting. Policy makers create a supportive environment in which practitioners and users can tell stories of their experience, and invite other people to learn from them. External evidence can also be used, but to begin a conversation and to initiate further experience-based evidence gathering. Advocates often refer to the importance of complex systems (Cairney 2012; Geyer and Cairney 2015), an inability to control delivery and policy outcomes, and the need to create new and bespoke evidence through practice or experiential learning. *My Home Life* (Scotland) is a key example (Dewar, Cook and Barrie 2014: 5).

The third approach relates to the improvement method and development of 'collaboratives'. The Scottish Government and ESRC (2013) refer explicitly to 'improvement methodologies' and 'collaboratives' as the way forward in the use of evidence to deliver policy. Advocates make reference to a process in which they identify promising interventions and encourage trained practitioners to adapt and experiment with the interventions in their area and gather data on their experience (Cairney 2015: 5). A discussion about how to scale up involves a mix of personal reflection on one's own project and a coordinated process of data gathering: people are asked for 'contextual' evidence for the success of their own programmes, but in a way that can be compared with others. The *Early Years Collaborative* (EYC) is a key example (Institute for Healthcare Improvement 2003: 1; Housden 2014: 68; Scottish Government 2014: 38–40, 53; Cairney 2015: 10).

All three models show some promise as vehicles to turn a broad aim, prevention and early intervention into concrete policy interventions with measurable objectives and outcomes. Yet, they also involve very different choices about the correct balance between central direction and local autonomy, and regarding the extent to which we should select a hierarchy of good evidence-gathering methods. To all intents and purposes, the Scottish Government is allowing a 'thousand flowers to bloom', or encouraging methodological pluralism, rather than setting out a single solution to prevention.

Conclusion

Overall, we identify broad hopes that the Scottish Government could select social investment and prevention policies during a window of opportunity. Policy makers would pay high attention to the problems of employment and economic growth, as well as high inequalities, public services costs and low trust in politics; produce feasible solutions to each problem; and have the motive and opportunity to select social investment and prevention as the best solutions.

Yet, the actual development of policy suggests that policy makers paid attention to an ill-defined problem and produced solutions which proved to be too vague to operationalise in a simple way. In other words, we identify a window of opportunity to adopt vague solutions, social investment and prevention, to address a very broad and often ill-defined policy problem: invest in infrastructure and human capital to boost economic growth, reduce inequalities and service demand, and find new ways to make policy and deliver public services.

Both concepts were promoted strongly by the Scottish Government (2011b, 2013) as strategies to invest for the long term, reduce the provision of relatively expensive reactive or acute public services in favour of investment in human capital, and reduce socioeconomic inequalities. Consequently, they represent the ever-present potential for major advances in socioeconomic progress. The right kinds of investments, coupled with reduced inequalities, would be consistent with the SNP's economic and social policy to reduce costs and improve economic growth. Further, the prevention agenda is linked strongly to democratic and governance reform, accompanying the Scottish Government's move towards setting broad strategies and working in partnership with the public sector, its stakeholders and service users to devolve the details of policy delivery to local communities as part of its self-styled Scottish Approach to Policymaking.

As such, social investment and prevention perhaps represent the most significant public policy and policy-making agendas since devolution, but they have helped produce modest Scottish models. Social investment under devolution involves the development of some social partnerships, combined with a commitment to a form of targeted universalism to promote social solidarity and identify some populations in need of greater attention. Prevention under devolution involves some small-scale but significant experimentation in different ways to deliver the same ends. In health and social care, we see early intervention programmes driven by approaches associated with evidence-based medicine. In care for older people, there is greater evidence of a storytelling approach built more on governance principles. In early years policy, the Scottish Government has placed great emphasis on collaboratives to combine some commitment to evidence with high levels of local autonomy. Overall, the Scottish model of social investment and prevention, under devolution, is one of pragmatism and experimentation.

7 Getting to a Wealthier and Fairer Scotland

Michael Keating and Robert Liñeira

The problem

The chapters in this book have focused on policies to fulfil the declared ambition of the Scottish Government to achieve a wealthier and fairer nation. The aim is unexceptionable and supported by all parties, but notoriously difficult to achieve in practice. In line with international thinking, the Scottish Government has argued for a social investment approach and for preventive spending in order to secure the long-term future, drawing particularly on the experience of the Nordic states but also of other countries that appear to combine economic performance with social inclusion. Yet defining these concepts and putting them into practice is not easy. Long-term ambitions must compete with short-term pressures on spending. The needs of future generations must be set against those of the present. Investment in physical and human capital may not provide the immediate, tangible benefits that come from current spending. While social investment may address economic and social problems at the same time by expanding opportunities and bringing people into the well-paid part of the labour force, it does not in itself resolve the big issues of inequality. There is still a role to be played by redistribution, which implies winners and losers among individuals and groups. It is also inescapable that to achieve Nordic levels of public spending it is necessary to pay Nordic levels of taxation, which are higher than those currently prevailing in the UK.

In this chapter, we ask whether the support base for such a strategy exists. First, we examine public opinion in Scotland

and compare it with that in the UK as a whole. We find that there is support for universal public services but that a broader sense of solidarity has fallen over recent decades. Scotland is only slightly more egalitarian than the rest of the UK. Then we consider how support for social inclusion and equality might be built, drawing on experience elsewhere. Finally, we examine the institutions and competences that Scotland has following the three devolution acts of 1998, 2012 and 2016.

What does Scotland want?

The first question is whether the Scottish electorate actually does support the policies of growth and solidarity articulated by successive governments. There is a long-standing myth of Scotland as an egalitarian society, with opportunities for all (Hearn 2000; McCrone 2001). A myth, in this sense, is not a story that is false but rather a shared belief whose power is independent of its truth or falsehood. The Scottish egalitarian myth is a recurrent one, from the old idea of the 'lad o' pairts', rising from humble beginnings to good fortune, often through the education system, to the belief in the 1980s that Scotland had been uniquely resistant to the policies of Margaret Thatcher. Perhaps more effort has been put into challenging this myth than ever was put into promoting it. Scotland in the industrial era of the nineteenth and twentieth centuries was an unequal society with sharp class divisions. Evidence from the 1980s in fact showed that, while the Scots had not been converted to Thatcherism, neither had most voters in England; the difference was that in Scotland opposition could be articulated around the national question, leading to a revival of the historic home rule movement and the achievement of devolution in 1999. Similarly, opposition to austerity and support for traditional social democracy were critical factors in extending support for independence into the working class and marginalised communities in the referendum of 2014.

Whether Scots are actually egalitarian is an empirical question which we can consider in two parts. The first is whether Scottish voters are egalitarian and supportive of a high-spending and high-taxation regime. The second, relevant in the context of devolution, is whether they are more supportive of public spending, and its implications for taxation, than those in the rest of the UK. Studies over the years have suggested that Scots are only slightly more egalitarian than people elsewhere in the UK (Brown et al. 1999). Rosie and Bond (2007) concur and add that Scots may be closer in their attitudes to people in the north of England, suggesting that it is southern England that is the outlier.

Evidence for attitudes to inequality and on levels of taxation, public spending and priorities is available from the British and Scottish Social Attitudes Survey over recent decades, and from our own survey conducted around the Scottish independence referendum (Henderson and Liñeira 2017). Figure 7.1 shows the responses to a rather general question as to whether the income gap is too large or too small; the figure represents the net support for the proposition that it is too high (those agreeing minus those disagreeing). When the question is put in this way there is massive support for the proposition that the gap is too large, again with only a slightly higher figure in Scotland.

A rather more difficult question is what people are prepared to do about this in the concrete as surveys have consistently shown that there is a difference between the numbers who think that inequality is too great and the numbers of people willing to act on it (Orton and Rowlingson 2007). Figure 7.2 shows levels of support for increasing taxation and spending

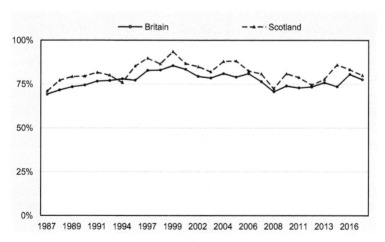

Figure 7.1 Attitudes towards the income gap. Percentage saying it is too large minus percentage saying it is too small.

Source: British Social Attitudes Survey (British and Scottish samples).

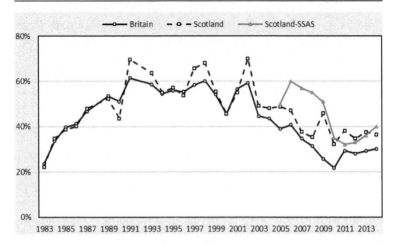

Figure 7.2 Net support for increased taxation and spending.

Note: The figure shows the percentage which supports the 'increase taxes and spend more' option minus the percentage which supports the 'reduce taxes and spend less' option.

Source: NatCen's British Social Attitudes Survey (British and Scottish samples) and ScotCen's Scottish Social Attitudes Survey (SSAS).

between 1983 and 2013. This indicator is at the core of the left–right division, showing the preference for more or less government intervention in the social and economic life through spending and taxation. There are three lessons here. One is that policy preferences move in reaction to changes of government. During the Conservative 1980s and into the 1990s net, support for increased taxation and spending reaches 60 per cent, but support fades away when the Labour Party reaches government in 1997. The tendency changes again in 2010 when the Conservatives are back in power. It has been suggested that policy preferences work as a thermostat, moving in the opposite direction to government policy: the electorate would signal the need to cool things when they get 'too hot' under Labour by supporting less taxation and spending, or would express that they are getting 'too cold' under Conservative administrations by demanding more government intervention (Soroka and Wlezien, 2010; Bartle, Avellaneda and Stimson 2011).

The second lesson is that there has always been a stronger preference for a stronger government intervention than the opposite

(the positive numbers show that the support for increased spending and taxation has always been greater than the support for
its reduction), although the support for increased taxation and
spending under the Cameron years is substantially lower than
the similar demand under the Thatcher administration, which
could indicate a long-term decline in support for redistribution
policies. Finally, while Scotland persistently diverges from the
rest of the UK, what is striking is the way in which British and
Scottish attitudes move in line with each other, although since
devolution there has been a slight tendency for Scottish respondents to take a less harsh attitude to welfare spending.[1]

Figure 7.3 shows the relative levels of support in 2014, again
indicating less opposition in Scotland towards welfare spending.

All of this would suggest a persistent tendency to greater
social solidarity in Scotland but not so large as to underpin a

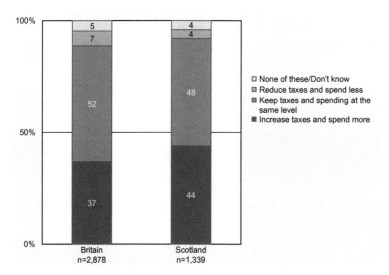

Figure 7.3 Preferences on taxation and government spending.

Note: Survey question: 'About the government choosing between these
three options. Which do you think it should choose? Reduce taxes and
spend less on health, education and social benefits OR keep taxes and
spending on these services at the same level as now OR increase taxes
and spend more on health, education and social benefits?'

Source: British Social Attitudes Survey 2014 and Scottish Social Attitudes
Survey 2014.

radically different policy stance. The biggest differences, moreover, are not between Scotland and the rest of the UK but among
the services for which people might be prepared to pay more.
Some public services are universal, benefiting all equally and
used by all at some time in their lives. These include health and
education, which are highly valued and for which there is strong
support for public provision. It is quite easy to find majorities
prepared, at least in principle, to pay more for these, as long as
they were assured that the money would be hypothecated; that
is, spent only on the service in question. Table 7.1 indicates that
roughly equal proportions of people in Britain as a whole and
in Scotland might pay more for these, but not for anything else.
Table 7.2 also suggests that substantial numbers would pay
more for the NHS specifically. Support for such services can be
explained by self-interest, as citizens gain directly from them.
They are a form of collective consumption, which partially
displaces private consumption. They can also be considered as
social investment, enhancing human capital and yielding wider
economic and social benefits.

It is another matter where explicitly redistributive items are
concerned; that is, items where citizens are invited to contribute to others. The founding principle of the welfare state was
a system of social insurance, to cover contingencies that any
of us might face at some time, including illness, old age and

Table 7.1 Hypothecated taxes, NHS taxes (preferences on extra
spending, % multichoice).

	Britain	Scotland	Difference
Health	75	77	−2
Education	61	58	3
Housing	19	21	−2
Help for industry	8	10	−1
Police and Prisons	8	7	1
Public transport	5	5	0
Roads	7	9	−2
Social Security	6	8	−2
Defence	1	0	0
None of these	1	1	0

Note: Survey question: 'Here are some items of government spending. Which of
them, if any, would be your next highest priority for extra spending?'

Source: British Social Attitudes Survey 2014 (British and Scottish samples)

Table 7.2 Support for funding the NHS at the expense of other services.

	Britain %	Scotland %
Yes	38	40
No	59	56
Don't know	3	4
n	2,878	252

Note: Survey question: 'Would you be willing for the government to spend less money on other public services, such as education, transport or policing, to maintain current NHS services?'

Source: British Social Attitudes Survey 2014 (British and Scottish samples)

unemployment. In this way self-interest and the social interest could coincide as benefits could potentially accrue to the individuals who were at any time contributing. It displaced an older idea about welfare as support for the poor, seen as a distinct category of the population. That, in turn, was entangled with historic distinctions between the 'deserving' and the 'undeserving' poor. So widows, the elderly and children might be seen as deserving while able-bodied adults were not. At times of full employment, the distinction faded as unemployment was temporary and cyclical, even helping the economy by encouraging labour mobility.

In recent years, these distinctions have reappeared, in the language used by politicians to contrast 'strivers' with 'skivers', or portrayals of the unemployed as people who cannot be bothered to get out of their beds in the morning. Figure 7.4, measuring support for the proposition that people are exploiting the benefits system, captures this change clearly. There is sympathy for the unemployed during the 1980s but this diminishes with the economic recovery in both Scotland and the rest of Britain. The recession resulting from the global economic crisis of 2008, however, generates only a small revival of sympathy, reflecting the long-term harshening of views, as well, perhaps, as the fact that this recession produced a reduction in incomes rather than mass unemployment. Once again, Scotland is only slightly more sympathetic.

The same picture emerges in Figure 7.5, which asks people whether government should spend more on the poor even if it

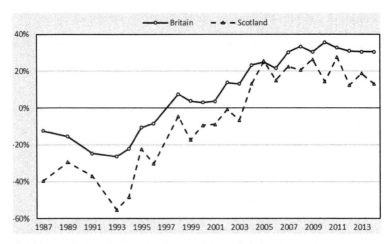

Figure 7.4 Net support for the idea: 'If welfare benefits weren't so generous, people would learn to stand on their own two feet.'

Note: The figure shows the percentage who agree with the statement minus the percentage of those who disagree.

Source: British Social Attitudes Survey (British and Scottish samples).

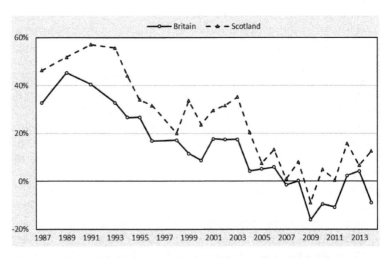

Figure 7.5 Net support for increased spending on benefits for the poor.

Note: The figure shows the percentage who agree with spending more money on welfare benefits for the poor, even if it leads to higher taxes, minus those who disagree.

Source: British Social Attitudes Survey (British and Scottish samples).

leads to higher taxes. Levels of solidarity with the poor are lower than in the 1980s, with only a small recovery after 2008.

Again, when asked whether unemployment benefits are too low, we see the falling off between the 1980s and the 2000s (Figure 7.6). The sustained and continued decline in support that Figures 7.4, 7.5 and 7.6 show for benefits suggests that an important part of the trend may be related to generational turnover; that is, the new British cohorts are much more reluctant to support these policy transfers than the old cohorts they are replacing (Orton and Rowlingson 2007). In this case, the difference between Scotland and the rest of the UK has diminished significantly.

It appears, then, that there is support in Scotland for universal services and potentially for social investment but less for explicitly redistributive policies and welfare as it is now defined. The next question is whether Scots really want Scotland to strike out on its own, irrespective of what happens in the rest of the UK. Here we encounter a paradox.

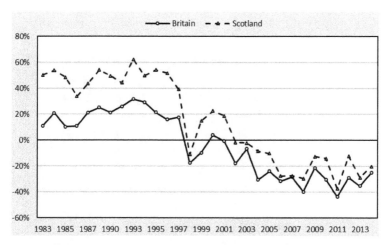

Figure 7.6 Net support for the idea that unemployment benefits are too low.

Note: The figure shows the percentage of those who say that benefits are too low minus the percentage of those who stay that benefits are too high.

Source: British Social Attitudes Survey (British and Scottish samples)

The devolution paradox

Devolution has been a long journey. The initial allocation of powers to the Scottish Parliament covered large areas of domestic policy, with the notable exceptions of taxation and welfare. Scotland could make big decisions about the organisation of its public services, but the large distributive issues remained at the centre. Surveys since then have consistently shown that most voters want Scotland to have more powers and specifically powers over taxation and welfare. In the independence referendum of 2014, Scottish voters were offered an apparently clear choice between independence and union, but during the long campaign the difference seemed to diminish as the SNP presented a version of 'independence-lite' including a currency union and common institutions, while the unionists offered more devolution. This was done in the knowledge that most voters were in the middle of the spectrum, wanting control over most domestic policies but not full independence. Our own surveys bear out this picture. Figure 7.7 shows support for the Scottish Government taking the decisions in most domestic policy spheres, including matters already devolved like

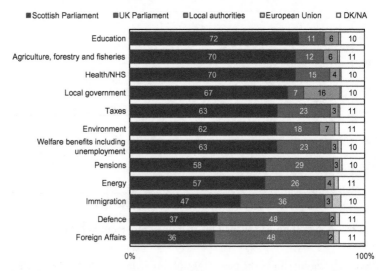

Figure 7.7 Which level of government should make the decisions?

Source: Henderson and Liñeira 2017.

education, agriculture and fisheries, local government and the environment, but also reserved matters such as welfare, pensions and energy.

Given the option of shared control, however, some electors would like both levels of government to be responsible for domestic policies, even including those already completely devolved like primary and secondary education, as shown in Figure 7.8.

All this would suggest that there might be a support base for a distinctive Scottish welfare settlement with its own balance of services and taxation and a capacity for redistribution through the welfare system. On the other hand, when people in Scotland are asked whether they would like policies to differ from those elsewhere in the UK, there is much less enthusiasm. This has been called the 'devolution paradox' and has been observed in a number of European countries (Bertelsmann Stiftung 2008; Centro de Investigaciones Sociológicas 2010; Curtice and Ormston 2011; Henderson et al. 2013). So, notwithstanding the fact that nearly two-thirds of people want the Scottish

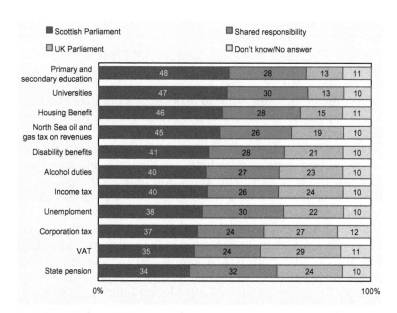

Figure 7.8 Who should make decisions?

Source: Henderson and Liñeira 2017.

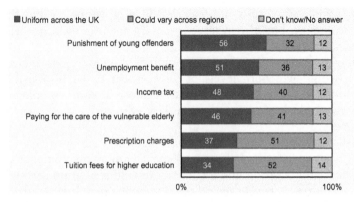

Figure 7.9 Support for policy variation across the UK.

Source: Henderson and Liñeira 2017.

Parliament to control welfare and unemployment benefits (Figure 7.7), more than half want them to be the same as in the rest of the UK (Figure 7.9).

The same applies to levels of taxation. In spite of widespread support for devolution of tax powers, some 43 per cent of our respondents wanted taxes to be set at the same levels as elsewhere in the UK, and only 17 per cent supported increasing them in the way that would be required to match the Nordic idea (Figure 7.10).

It is difficult to know what to make of this persistent finding, which appears to be contradictory. Some light is thrown on the matter in our survey finding reported in Figure 7.11, showing that a majority of people wanted pensions and a plurality wanted welfare benefits to be funded at the UK level, in contrast to health and education. This appears to reflect a recognition of the need for sharing over a wider area and the potential weakness of Scotland's public finances.

It may also be that people are less concerned with making policy differently than in ownership of the policy and the feeling that it is locally controlled. There is also the likelihood that people are reluctant to accept that increases in spending in some fields will require either cuts elsewhere or increases in taxation. They may also look to having at least parity with the rest of the UK in each particular service, fearing that otherwise they might lose out, and are in favour of levelling up. It seems

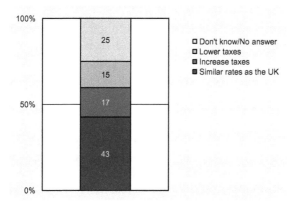

Figure 7.10 What the Scottish Parliament should do with its new taxation powers.

Source: Henderson and Liñeira 2017.

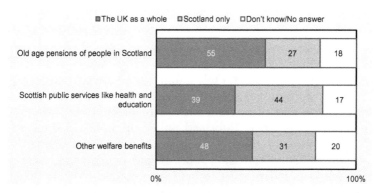

Figure 7.11 How should services be financed?

Source: Henderson and Liñeira 2017.

unlikely that were they asked whether they wanted levels of services reduced to UK levels in those fields in which they are higher, they would agree.

Building support

Another interpretation of the findings is that people do not have fixed preferences as to public policies but rather general orientations about the goals to achieve, which might be satisfied in different ways. The essential preconditions for mass political thinking are that the matter must demand neither detailed knowledge nor analytical skills from the public. As a result, thoughts about political substance tend to focus on values, goals and performance rather than on specific policies. The lack of familiarity with specific policy alternatives may render the people's answers very inconsistent as a result of question-wording effects; the latest political events may also prompt individuals to prefer one or another policy alternative as respondents tends to respond to survey questions from the 'top-of-their-minds' (Zaller and Feldman 1992), particularly if they are unfamiliar with or do not have a firm opinion on the issue.

In consequence, only in those circumstances when there has been an intense debate about specific policy alternatives might the voter have an opinion on his or her preferences. However, not even in these contexts can public policy be the mere product of aggregated individual preferences since they are so contradictory that expenditure implications would never add up.

There is, moreover, a difference in asking individual respondents for their individual views, and debating matters in a social and institutional context. Only a minority of altruists will actually want to give away some of their money to others. If this is presented as part of a wider social bargain they may respond differently in practice. Informed public opinion is not merely an aggregation of these individual preferences but rather is formed in an institutional, political and deliberative context in which both individual and broader societal needs are taken into account. The survey context, then, is not the same as the context voters face when making their electoral choice. Parties present packages of policies and taxes to the electors and ask for support in return.

Rothstein (2001), Rothstein and Steinmo (2013) and others have argued that the success of the Nordic countries' policy choices is to have aligned the interests of individual citizens with those of the wider society through having the right institutions that shape the political debate. This requires that policies be seen as just; that all contribute to them; and that they are delivered in a fair and non-corrupt way. This explanation does not rely on individuals spontaneously being altruistic. Nor does it rely on cultural stereotypes about the characteristics of different societies or ingrained levels of solidarity. Rather, it stems from experience of institutions that work and deliver public goods. A key ingredient is the existence of universal public services, used by the whole of society, so aligning private and public interests and creating shared support for high levels of service provision. If some citizens can ride free or opt out, such support will be lacking. This suggests that the Scottish preference for universal rather than selective services, often criticised as 'middle-class benefits' or 'something for nothing', may point in the right direction but only if it is underpinned by a system of progressive taxation that funds it adequately with contributions according to means.

It may also happen that support follows, rather than precedes, policies as people appreciate their benefits. The problem then arises of how to generate support in the first place in a context in which people do not know whether they will personally benefit or whether others will contribute their share. Moving from a relatively low-tax and inegalitarian society to a more egalitarian one might be a difficult process, even if there would be widespread benefits in the end. The wide support for spending on health and education at least suggests that, where a service is almost universal and respected, it can sustain public support.

There is some prospect for generating support for a social investment strategy based on public services, notably in health and education. There is less support, however, for explicitly redistributive policies and, especially, for welfare. The Scottish Government's relabelling of welfare as 'social security' (Chapter 4) is a way of combatting distinctions between universal services and welfare and between the deserving and the undeserving, but is less easy to sell as social investment. Social investment on its own may not be an effective way of addressing inequality unless accompanied by other measures to secure benefits for the most disadvantaged. Indeed, it may even increase the premium for those possessed of most human capital (Rhodes 2013). On the other hand, taxation alone may not be the best way to address inequality, given the way in which people can avoid higher taxes (Chapter 3). This all suggests that measures to enhance human capital and opportunities for the disadvantaged may be the best way forward.

Institutions and powers

Institutions and the allocation of competences remain critically important. First, they can equip the Scottish Government with the tools to enhance growth and secure more equality. Second, they can create the incentive for public and private actors to act in a way that secures these aims. Third, they can align private and wider social interests in positive-sum social compromises.

Before the Scotland Act (2016), there was the prospect that the fiscal benefit from social investment measures by the Scottish Government would flow to Westminster. For example, expenditure on childcare might expand the workforce and generate more taxes but the spending would be done by the Scottish Government while the income tax from the new workers would go to London, as happened in the case of Quebec (Chapter 5). The devolution of income tax on earned income partly resolves this problem, although National Insurance contributions still flow to Westminster. The assignment of half of VAT revenues to Scotland also provides an incentive to pro-growth policies that boost the tax base.

On the other hand, the devolution of welfare powers remains patchy, the result of a political compromise rather than a studied design. Scotland does not have the power to design its own welfare system but can only fill in gaps in the UK system. This can be very costly, given that Scottish taxpayers will still have to contribute to the UK benefits system as well as any new Scottish measures. The pattern of devolution also makes it difficult to align the benefits system with work incentives in new ways and link it to active labour market policies. The administration of the Work Programme, aimed at getting people into employment, is being devolved but not the wider welfare-to-work system as a whole. There has been widespread support in the voluntary sector for more wide-ranging devolution of welfare to enable a more comprehensive reform of the system. Within the trade unions there is also support for devolution of labour market policy to provide a better link to policies against social exclusion.

Indeed, one factor in increasing inequality appears to be the weakening of trade unions and collective bargaining. The Scottish Government has been more pro-trade union than its Westminster counterpart, but trade union and labour law remains reserved and there is a limited amount that can be done at the Scottish level. The lack of a Scottish level of collective bargaining means that it is difficult to trade off individual wage increases against the 'social wage' in order to provide for more collective consumption and investment (Chapter 2). This is further weakened by the decline of trade union membership, especially in the private sector, making social concertation and partnership more difficult. Scotland, like the UK as a whole, remains a liberal market rather than a coordinated market economy and the private sector is not used to, or favourably inclined towards, social concertation.

The scope for grand bargains at the Scottish level is thus limited and there is no magic formula for combining economic growth with social inclusion. The way forward is more likely to be, as outlined in Chapter 6, through experimental approaches to innovation; creating narratives (stories) of success; and collaborative policy making within individual sectors. The emphasis here is on the humdrum, rather than the heroic, style of policy making, building from experience but guided by wider aims and building policy capacity over time. A final conclusion remains inescapable, though: if Scotland wants a developed, social democratic, social investment welfare state, it will have to pay for it.

Note

1. The greater fluctuation in the Scottish figure from the British Social Attitudes Survey (BSAS) is the result of having a smaller sample; from 2005 the question is asked separately in the Scottish Social Attitudes Survey (SSAS) with a similar size to the British one.

References

Alesina, A. and Spolaore, E. (2003) *The Size of Nations*. Cambridge, MA: The MIT Press.

Amior, M., Crawford, G. and Tetlow, R. (2013) *Fiscal Sustainability of an Independent Scotland*. Institute for Fiscal Studies. Accessed at: https://www.ifs.org.uk/comms/r88.pdf

Atkinson A. (2015) *Inequality: What Can be Done?* London: Harvard University Press.

Auerbach, A., Gokhale, J. and Kotlikoff, L. (1991) Generational accounts: a meaningful alternative to deficit accounting. In D. Bradford (ed.) *Tax Policy and the Economy*, Vol. 5, Cambridge, MA: The MIT Press, pp. 55–110.

Autor, D. H., Levy, F. and Murnane, R. J. (2003) The skill content of recent technological change: an empirical exploration. *Quarterly Journal of Economics*, 116(4): 1279–1333.

Avdagic, S., Rhodes, M. and Visser, J. (2011) *Social Pacts in Europe: Emergence, Evolution and Institutionalization*. Oxford: Oxford University Press.

Azong, J. (2015) *Economic Policy, Childcare and the Unpaid Economy: Exploring Gender Equality in Scotland*. Accessed at: http://hdl.handle.net/1893/22827

Azong, J. and Wilińksa, M. (2016) Into a footnote: unpaid care work and the Equality Budget in Scotland. *European Journal of Women's Studies*. Accessed at http://ejw.sagepub.com/content/early/2016/04/17/1350506816643731.full.pdf+html

Bank of England (2012) *The Distributional Effects of Asset Purchases*. Bank of England Quarterly Bulletin 2012 Q3: 254–66.

Banting, K. (2005) Canada: nation-building in a federal welfare state. In H. Obinger, S. Leibfried and F. G. Castles (eds) *Federalism and the Welfare State: New World and European Experiences*. Cambridge: Cambridge University Press, pp. 89–137.

Bartle, J., Avellaneda, S. D. and Stimson, J. A. (2011) The policy mood and the moving centre. In N. Allen and J. Bartle (eds) *Britain at the Polls 2010*. London: Sage.

Beaujot, R., Du, C. J. and Ravanera, Z. (2013) Family policies in Quebec and the rest of Canada: implications for fertility, child-care, women's paid work, and child development indicators. *Canadian Public Policy*, 39(2): 221–39.

Béland, D. and Lecours, A. (2008) *Nationalism and Social Policy. The Politics of Territorial Solidarity*. Oxford: Oxford University Press.

Belfield, C., Cribb, J., Hood, A. and Joyce, R. (2015) *Living Standards, Poverty and Inequality in the UK: 2015*. Institute for Fiscal Studies, July. Accessed at: http://www.ifs.org.uk/uploads/publications/comms/R107.pdf

Bell, D. (2013) The Block Grant Adjustment. Paper to Finance Committee. Scottish Parliament. Accessed at: http:/www.scottish.parliament.uk/S4_FinanceCommittee/Scotland_Act_12.pdf

Bell, D. and Eiser, D. (2013) *Inequality in Scotland: Trends, Drivers and Implications for the Referendum Debate*. Stirling: Scottish Fiscal and Economic Studies. Accessed at: http://www.centreoncon stitutionalchange.ac.uk/sites/default/files/papers/inequality-paper-15-nov-final.pdf

Bell, D. and Eiser, D. (2014a) *Inequality in Scotland: Trends, Drivers, and Implications for the Independence Debate*. Edinburgh: ESRC Scottish Centre on Constitutional Change.

Bell, D. and Eiser, D. (2014b) *Scotland's Fiscal Future in the UK*. University of Stirling.

Bell, D. and Eiser, D. (2015a) The economic case for further fiscal decentralisation to Scotland: theoretical and empirical perspectives. *National Institute Economic Review*, 233(1): R27–R36.

Bell, D. and Eiser, D. (2015b) *Inequality in Scotland: What Can be Done?* Edinburgh: David Hume Institute. Accessed at: http://www.davidhumeinstitute.com/wp-content/uploads/2015/07/Inequality-in-Scotland.pdf

Bell D., Eiser D. and McGoldrick, M. (2014) *Inequality in Scotland: New Perspectives*. Edinburgh: David Hume Institute. Accessed at: http://www.davidhumeinstitute.com/wp-content/uploads/2015/01/Inequality-in-Scotland-New-Perspectives-Bell-et-al.pdf

Bell V., Joyce M., Liu Z. and Young, C. (2012) The distributional effects of asset purchases. *Bank of England Quarterly Bulletin*, Q3.

Bertelsmann Stiftung (2008) *Bürger und Föderalismus. Eine Umfage zur Roller der Bundeslander*. Gütersloh: Bertlesmann.

Billis, D. (1981) At risk of prevention. *Journal of Social Policy*, 10(3): 367–79.

Bjork-Eydal, G. (2012) Childcare policies at a crossroads: the case of

Iceland. In A.-T. Kjørholt and J. Qvortrup (eds) *The Modern Child and the Flexible Labour Market*. Basingstoke: Palgrave Macmillan, pp. 38–55.

Bonoli, G. (2007) Time matters: postindustrialization, new social risks, and welfare state adaptation in advanced industrial democracies. *Comparative Political Studies*, 40(5): 495–520.

Borchorst, A. (2009) Women friendly policy paradoxes? Childcare policies and gender equality visions in Scandinavia. In K. Melby, A.-B. Raun and C. C. Wettenberg (eds) *Gender Equality and Welfare Politics in Scandinavia: The Limits of Politics Ambition*. Bristol: The Policy Press.

Brandal, N., Bratberg, Ø. and Thorsen, D. E. (2013) *The Nordic Model of Social Democracy*. Basingstoke: Palgrave Macmillan.

Brandth, B. and Kvande, E. (2012) Free choice or gentle force? How can parental leave change gender practices? In A.-T. Kjørholt and J. Qvortrup (eds) *The Modern Child and the Flexible Labour Market*. Basingstoke: Palgrave Macmillan, pp. 56–70.

Briggs, A. (2000) The welfare state in historical perspective. In C. Pierson and F. G. Castles (eds) *The Welfare State: A Reader*. Cambridge: Polity Press.

Brown, A., McCrone, D., Paterson, L. and Surridge, P. (1999) *The Scottish Electorate: The 1997 General Election and Beyond*. Basingstoke: Macmillan.

Bryson, C., Kazimirksi, A. and Southwood, H. (2006) *Childcare and Early Years Provision: A Study of Parents' Use, Views and Experience*. National Centre for Social Research Research Report 723. London: Department of Education and Skills.

Budig, M. J., Misra, J. and Boeckmann, I. (2012) The motherhood penalty in cross-national perspective: the importance of work–family policies and cultural attitudes. *Social Politics*, 19(2): 163–93.

Butcher, T., Dickens, R. and Manning, A. (2012) *Minimum Wages and Wage Inequality: Some Theory and an Application to the UK*. CEP Discussion Paper 1177.

Cairney, P. (2009) Implementation and the governance problem. *Public Policy and Administration*, 24(4): 355–77.

Cairney, P. (2011) *The Scottish Political System Since Devolution*. Exeter: Imprint Academic.

Cairney, P. (2012) Complexity theory in political science and public policy. *Political Studies Review*, 10: 346–58.

Cairney, P. (2013) Territorial policy communities and the Scottish policy style: the case of compulsory education. *Scottish Affairs*, 82(Winter): 10–34.

Cairney, P. (2014) The territorialisation of interest representation in Scotland: did devolution produce a new form of group-government relations? *Territory, Politics, Governance*, 2(3): 303–21.

Cairney, P. (2015) Evidence-based best practice is more political than it looks: a case study of the 'Scottish Approach'. *Evidence and Policy*, Early View Open Access.

Cairney, P. (2016a) The Scottish Parliament Election 2016: another momentous event but dull campaign. *Scottish Affairs*, 25(3): 277–93.

Cairney, P. (2016b) *The Politics of Evidence-Based Policy Making*. London: Palgrave Pivot.

Cairney, P. and Jones, M. (2016) Kingdon's multiple streams approach: what is the empirical impact of this universal theory? *Policy Studies Journal*, 44(1): 37–58.

Cairney, P. and St Denny, E. (2015) Prevention is better than cure, so why isn't government policy more preventive? *Political Insight*, December: 12–15.

Cairney, P. and Widfeldt, A. (2015) Is Scotland a Westminster-style majoritarian democracy or a Scandinavian-style consensus democracy? A comparison of Scotland, the UK and Sweden. *Regional and Federal Studies*, 25(1): 1–18.

Cairney, P., Russell, S. and St Denny, E. (2016) The 'Scottish approach' to policy and policymaking: what issues are territorial and what are universal? *Policy and Politics*, 44(3): 333–50.

Centro de Investigaciones Sociológicas (CIS) (2010), *Barómetro Autonómico 2829*. Madrid: CIS.

Charlesworth, S. (2013) Women, work and industrial relations in Australia in 2012. *Journal of Industrial Relations*, 55(3): 371–85.

Cingano, F. (2014) *Trends in Income Inequality and its Impact on Economic Growth*. OECD Social, Employment and Migration Working Papers. DOI: 10.1787/1815199x

Cohen, M., March, J. and Olsen, J. (1972) A garbage can model of organizational choice. *Administrative Science Quarterly*, 17(1): 1–25.

Comerford, D. and Eiser, D. (2014) Constitutional change and inequality in Scotland. *Oxford Review of Economic Policy*, 30(2): 346–73.

Commission of the Future Delivery of Public Services (2011) *Report*. Edinburgh: Scottish Government. Accessed at: http://www.scotland.gov.uk/Resource/Doc/352649/0118638.pdf

Compston, H. (2002) The strange persistence of policy concertation. In S. Berger and H. Compston (eds) *Policy Concertation and Social Partnership in Western Europe*. New York/Oxford: Berghahn.

Cooke, P. and Morgan, K. (1998) *The Associational Economy. Firms, Regions, and Innovation*. Oxford: Oxford University Press.

Crouch, C. (2013) Class politics and the social investment welfare state. In M. Keating and D. McCrone (eds) *The Crisis of Social Democracy in Europe*. Edinburgh: Edinburgh University Press.

Crouch, C., Le Galès, P., Trigilia, C. and Voelzkow, H. (2001) *Local Production Systems in Europe. Rise or Demise?* Oxford: Oxford University Press.

Curtice, J. and Ormston, R. (2011) *Ready to Take Another Leap? Public Opinion on how Scotland Should be Governed.* Edinburgh: Scottish Centre for Social Research.

Dabla-Norris, E., Kochhar, K., Suphaphiphat, N., Ricka, F. and Tsounta, E. (2015) *Causes and Consequences of Income Inequality: A Global Perspective.* International Monetary Fund, Staff Discussion Notes, No 15/13. Accessed at: https://www.imf.org/external/pubs/ft/sdn/2015/sdn1513.pdf

Darby, J., Ferret, B. and Wooton, I. (2014) Firm location, natural geography and the corporation tax debate. *Fraser Economic Commentary*, 38(1): 94–9.

Dewar, B., Cook, F. and Barrie, K. (2014) *Final Report: Exploring the Experiences of Staff, Residents and Families in Care Homes to Support the Design of New Care Homes in West Dumbarton.* Paisley: University of the West of Scotland. Accessed at: http://myhomelife uws ac uk/scotland/wp-content/uploads/2014/06/Report-West-DunbartonshireFINAL pdf

Duvander, A.-Z. and Ferrarini, T. (2013) *Sweden's Family Policy under Change: Past, Present, Future.* SPaDE Working Paper Number 8, Stockholm University.

Elson, D., Balakrishnan, R. and Heintz, J. (2013) Public finance, maximum available resources and human rights. In C. Harvey, A. Nolan and R. O'Connell (eds) *Human Rights and Public Finance: Budget Analysis and the Advancement of Economic and Social Rights.* Oxford: Hart Publishing.

Elvidge, J. (2011) *Northern Exposure: Lessons from the First Twelve Years of Devolved Government in Scotland.* London: Institute for Government. Accessed at: http://www instituteforgovernment org.uk/sites/default/files/publications/Northern%20Exposure pdf

Esping-Andersen, G. (1999) *Social Foundations of Post-Industrial Economies.* Oxford: Oxford University Press.

European Union, Directorate General for Internal Policies (2015) *Wage and Income Inequality in the European Union.* January. Accessed at: http://www.europarl.europa.eu/RegData/etudes/STUD/2015/536294/IPOL_STU(2015)536294_EN.pdf

Expert Working Group on Welfare (2013) *First Report.* Edinburgh: Scottish Government.

Family and Childcare Trust (2014) *The 2014 Scottish Childcare Report.* London: Family and Childcare Trust. Accessed at: http://www.familyandchildcaretrust.org/Handlers/Download.ashx?IDMF=4b29ac82-730c-46c4-8ce2-a18c83842950

Ferrera, M. (2005) *The New Boundaries of Welfare.* Oxford: Oxford University Press.

Ferrera, M. and Rhodes, M. (2000) Recasting European welfare states: an introduction. *West European Politics*, 23(2): 1–10.

Fortin, P., Godbout, L. and St-Cerny, S. (2012) *The Impact of Quebec's Universal Low Fee Child Care Program on Female Labour Force Participation, Domestic Income and Government Budgets.* Working Paper 2012/02. Chaire de recherche en fiscalité et finances publiques, University of Sherbrooke.

Gallagher, A. (2013) The politics of childcare provisioning: a geographical perspective. *Geography Compass*, 7(2): 161–71.

Gallego, R. and Subirats, J. (2011) Comporta el desplegament autonòmic un augment de les desigualtats a Espanya? Descentralització, polítiques de benestar i justicia social. In R. Gallego and J. Subirats (eds) *Autonomies i desigualtats a Espanya: Perceptions, evolució social i polítiques de benestar.* Barcelona: Institut d'Estudis Autonómics.

Gallego, R. and Subirats, J. (2012) Spanish and regional welfare systems: policy innovation and multi-level governance. *Regional & Federal Studies*, 22(3): 269–88.

GERS (2013) *Government Expenditure and Revenue Scotland 2012–13.* Edinburgh: Scottish Government. Accessed at: http://www.scot land.gov.uk/Topics/Statistics/Browse/Economy/GERS

GERS (2016) *Government Expenditure and Revenue Scotland 2015–16.* Edinburgh: Scottish Government. Accessed at: http://www.gov. scot/Publications/2016/08/2132

Geyer, R. and Cairney, P. (eds) (2015) *Handbook on Complexity and Public Policy.* Cheltenham: Edward Elgar.

Gibb, K. (2013) The Economics of the Land and Buildings Transactions Tax. Paper to Finance Committee. Edinburgh: Scottish Parliament. Accessed at: http:/www.scottish.parliament.uk/S4_ FinanceCommittee/Scotland_Act_12.pdf

Gilmartin, M., Learmonth, D., McGregor, P. G., Swales, J. K. and Turner, K. R. (2013) Regional policy spillovers: demand-side policy simulation with labour market constraints in a two-region computable general equilibrium framework. *Environment and Planning A*, 45(4), 814–34.

Gough, I. (2013) *Understanding Prevention Policy: A Theoretical Approach.* London: NEF. Accessed at: http://eprints.lse.ac.uk/ 47951/1/Understanding%20prevention%20policy%20(lsero).pdf

Grace, J. (2011) Gender and institutions of multi-level government: child care and social policy debates in Canada. In M. L. Krook and F. Mckay (eds) *Gender, Politics and Institutions: Towards a Feminist Institutionalism.* Basingstoke: Palgrave Macmillan, pp. 95–111.

Greener, I. (2005) The potential of path dependence in political studies. *Politics*, 25(1): 62–72.

Grönlund, A. and Öun, I. (2010) Rethinking work-family conflict: dual-earner policies, role conflict and role expansion in Western Europe. *Journal of European Social Policy*, 20(3): 179–95.

Haas, L. and Rostgaard, T. (2011) Fathers' rights to paid parental leave in the Nordic countries: consequences for the gendered division of leave. *Community, Work and Family*, 14(2): 177–95.

Hall, P. A. and Soskice, D. (2001) An introduction to varieties of capitalism. In P. A. Hall and D. Soskice (eds) *Varieties of Capitalism: The Institutional Foundations of Comparative Advantage*. Oxford: Oxford University Press.

Harrigan, F., McGregor P. G., Dourmashkin, N., Perman R., Swales, K. and Yin, Y. P. (1991) AMOS: A macro-micro model of Scotland. *Economic Modelling*, 8(4): 424–79.

Harvey, M. (2015) A social democratic future? Political and institutional hurdles in Scotland. *Political Quarterly*, 86(2), Spring.

Hearn, J. (2000) *Claiming Scotland: National Identity and Liberal Culture*. Edinburgh: Edinburgh University Press.

Heckman, J. J. (2008) Schools, skills, and synapses. *Economic Inquiry*, 46: 289–324.

Hemerijck, A. (2013) *Changing Welfare States*. Oxford: Oxford University Press.

Henderson, A., Jeffery, C. and Wincott, D. (eds) (2013) *Citizenship after the Nation-State*. Basingstoke: Macmillan.

Henderson, A., Jeffery, C., Wincott, D. and Wyn Jones, R. (2013) Reflections on the Devolution Paradox: a comparative examination of multi-level citizenship. *Regional Studies*, 47(3): 303–22.

Henderson, A. and Liñeira, R. (2017) Smith Commission Survey: Devolution Preferences in Scotland, England and Wales. [Data Collection]. Colchester, Essex: UK Data Archive.

Hermannsson, K., Lecca, P., Lisenkova, K., McGregor, P. G. and Swales, J. K. (2014) The regional economic impact of more graduates in the labour market: a 'micro-to-macro' analysis for Scotland. *Environment and Planning A*, 42(2): 471–87.

HM Government/Scottish Government (2016) *The Agreement Between the Scottish Government and the United Kingdom Government on the Scottish Government's Fiscal Framework*. Available at: https://www.gov.uk/government/publications/the-agreement-between-the-scottish-government-and-the-united-kingdom-government-on-the-scottish-governments-fiscal-framework

Holtham, G. (2010) *Final Report of the Independent Commission on Funding and Finance*. Welsh Assembly Government.

Hooghe, L., Marks, G. and Schakel, A. J. (2008) Regional authority in 42 democracies, 1950–2006: a measure and five hypotheses. *Regional and Federal Studies, Special Issue*, 18(2–3): 111–302.

Housden, P. (2014) This is us. *Civil Service Quarterly*, 16 April. Accessed at: https://quarterly blog gov uk/2014/04/16/this-is-us/

Huber, E., Ragin, C. and Stephens, J. (1993) Social democracy,

Christian democracy, constitutional structure and the welfare state. *The American Journal of Sociology*, 99(3): 711–49.

Huff, A. D. and Cotte, J. (2013) Complexities of consumption: the case of childcare. *The Journal of Consumer Affairs*, 47(1): 72–97.

Hunter-Blackburn, L. (2014) The fairest of them all? Mimeo. Accessed at: http://www.docs.hss.ed.ac.uk/education/creid/Projects/34ii_d_ESRCF_WP3.pdf

Institute for Healthcare Improvement (2003) *The Breakthrough Series: IHIs Collaborative Model for Achieving Breakthrough Improvement*. Boston, MA: Institute for Healthcare Improvement. Available at: http://www ihi org/resources/Pages/IHIWhitePapers/TheBreakthroughSeriesIHIsCollaborativeModelforAchievingBreakthroughImprovement aspx

Jeffery, C. (2002) Uniformity and diversity in policy provision: insights from the US, Germany and Canada. In J. Adams and P. Robinson (eds) *Devolution in Practice: Public Policy Differences within the UK*. London: IPPR.

Jones, M. D., Peterson, H. L., Pierce, J. J., Herweg, N., Bernal, A., Raney, H. L. and Zahariadis, N. (2016) A river runs through it: a multiple streams meta review. *Policy Studies Journal*, 44(1): 13–36.

Katzenstein, P. J. (1985) *Small States in World Markets: Industrial Policy in Europe*. Ithaca: Cornell University Press.

Kazepov, Y. and Barberis, E. (2008) La dimensione territoriale delle politiche sociali in Europa: alcune riflessioni sui processi di rescaling e governance. *Revista delle Politiche Sociali*, 3: 51–78.

Keating, M. (1998) *The New Regionalism in Western Europe: Territorial Restructuring and Political Change*. Cheltenham: Edward Elgar.

Keating, M. (2009) Social citizenship, solidarity and welfare in regionalized and plurinational states. *Citizenship Studies*, 13(5): 501–13.

Keating, M. (2010) *The Government of Scotland. Public Policy Making after Devolution*, 2nd edition. Edinburgh: Edinburgh University Press.

Keating, M. (2013) *Rescaling the European State. The Making of Territory and the Rise of the Meso*. Oxford: Oxford University Press.

Keating, M. (ed.) (2017) *Debating Scotland. Issues of Independence and Union in the 2014 Referendum*. Oxford: Oxford University Press.

Keating, M. and Harvey, M. (2014) *Small Nations in a Big World. What Scotland Can Learn*. Edinburgh: Luath.

Keating, M. and Wilson, A. (2014) Regions with regionalism? The rescaling of interest groups in six European States. *European Journal of Political Research*, 53(4): 840–57.

Keating M., Cairney, P. and Hepburn, E. (2009) Territorial policy communities and devolution in the United Kingdom. *Cambridge Journal of Regions, Economy and Society*, 2(1): 51–66.

Keating, M., Loughlin, J. and Deschouwer, K. (2003) *Culture,*

Institutions and Economic Development. A Study of Eight European Regions. Cheltenham: Edward Elgar.

Keck, W. and Saraceno, C. (2013) The impact of different social-policy frameworks on social inequalities among women in the European Union: the labour-market participation of mothers. *Social Politics: International Studies in Gender, State & Society,* 20(3): 297–328.

Kingdon, J. (1984) *Agendas, Alternatives and Public Policies.* New York: Harper Collins.

Kingdon, J. (1995) *Agendas, Alternatives and Public Policies.* London: Longman.

Kotlikoff, L. (1992) *Generational Accounting: Knowing Who Pays, and When, for What We Spend.* New York: The Free Press.

Kottelenberg, M. J. and Lehrer, S. F. (2013) New evidence on the impacts of access to and attending universal child-care in Canada. *Canadian Public Policy,* 39(2): 263–85.

Krapf, S. (2014) Who uses public childcare for 2-year-old children? Coherent family policies and usage patterns in Sweden, Finland and Western Germany. *International Journal of Social Welfare,* 23(1): 25–40.

Krugman, P. (2011) The new economic geography, now middle aged. *Regional Studies,* 45(1): 1–7.

Layard R., Nickell S. and Jackman R. (1991) *Unemployment: Macroeconomic Performance and the Labour Market.* Oxford: Oxford University Press.

Lecca, P., McGregor, P. G. and Swales, J. K. (2012a) Balanced Budget Government Spending in a Small Open Regional Economy. *ERSA Conference Papers* ersa12p1009, European Regional Science Association.

Lecca, P., McGregor, P. G. and Swales, J. K. (2012b) The impact of a devolved corporation tax to Scotland. Scottish Institute for Research in Economics (SIRE) Conference on International Business Taxation, Glasgow. University of Strathclyde, unpublished manuscript.

Lecca, P., McGregor, P. G. and Swales, J. K. (2014) Balanced budget current and capital government expenditure: the likely impact of greater fiscal autonomy for Scotland. University of Strathclyde, unpublished manuscript.

Lecca, P., McGregor, P. G. and Swales, J. K. (2015) Scotland – no detriment, no danger; the interregional impact of a balanced budget regional fiscal expansion. Accessed at: http://strathprints.strath.ac.uk/55430/

Lecca, P., McGregor, P. G., Swales, J. K. and Yin, Y. (2014) Balanced budget multipliers for small open regions within a federal system: evidence from the Scottish variable rate of income tax. *Journal of Regional Science,* 53: 402–21.

Levell, P., Roantree, B. and Shaw, J. (2015) *Redistribution from a Lifetime Perspective*. Institute for Fiscal Studies Working Paper 15/27

Lindley, J. and Machin, S. (2013) Wage inequality in the Labour years. *Oxford Review of Economic Policy*, 29(1): 165–77.

Liñeira, R., Henderson, A. and Delaney, L. (2017) Voters' response to the campaign. In M. Keating (ed.) Debating Scotland. Issues of Independence and Union in the 2014 Referendum. Oxford: Oxford University Press, pp. 165–90.

Lisenkova, K., Sanchez-Martinez, M. and Sefton, J. (2015) *The Sustainability of Scottish Public Finances: a Generational Accounting Approach*. NIESR Discussion Paper No. 456.

McCarthy, D., Sefton, J. and Weale, M. (2011) *Generational Accounts for the United Kingdom*. NIESR Discussion Paper No. 377.

McCrone, D. (2001) *Understanding Scotland. The Sociology of a Nation*, 2nd edition. London: Routledge.

McCrone, G. (2014) Submission to the Finance Committee of the Scottish Parliament, 7 May.

McEwen, N. (2006) *Nationalism and the State. Welfare and Identity in Scotland and Quebec*. Brussels: PIE/Peter Lang.

McEwen, N. and Moreno, L. (eds) (2005) *The Territorial Politics of Welfare*. London: Routledge.

MacRae, H. (2010) Multiple policy scales and the development of parental leave schemes in Germany. In M. Sawer and J. Vickers (eds) *Federalism, Feminism and Multi-Level Governance*. Farnham: Ashgate, pp. 127–39.

Mahon, R. and Collier, C. (2010) Navigating the shoals of Canadian federalism: childcare advocacy. In M. Sawer and J. Vickers (eds) *Federalism, Feminism and Multi-Level Governance*. Farnham: Ashgate, pp. 51–66.

Mankiw, N. G. (2013) Defending the one percent. *The Journal of Economic Perspectives*, 27(3): 21–34.

Marshall, A. (1920) *Principles of Economics*. London: Macmillan.

Marshall, T. H. (1950) *Citizenship and Social Class*. Cambridge: Cambridge University Press.

Marshall, T. H. (1992) *Citizenship and Social Class*. London: Pluto.

Midwinter, A., Keating, M. and Mitchell, J. (1991) *Politics and Public Policy in Scotland*. London: Macmillan.

Miller, H. and Pope, T. (2016) *The Changing Composition of UK Tax Revenues*. Institute for Fiscal Studies, Briefing Note 182.

Mischke, M. (2011) Types of public family support: a cluster analysis of 15 European countries. *Journal of Comparative Policy Analysis: Research and Practice*, 13(4): 443–56.

Mishra, R. (1999) *Globalization and the Welfare State*. Cheltenham: Edward Elgar.

Mooney, G. and Scott, G. (2015) The 2014 Scottish independence debate: questions of social welfare and social justice. *Journal of Poverty and Social Justice*, 23(1): 5–16.

Moreno, L. (2003) Europeanization, mesogovernments and safety nets. *European Journal of Political Research*, 42(2): 185–99.

National Records Office (2015, 29 October) *Projected Population of Scotland (2014-based). National Population Projections by Sex and Age, with UK Comparisons.* Accessed at: http://www. nrscotland.gov.uk/statistics-and-data/statistics/statistics-by-theme/ population/population-projections/population-projections-scotla nd/2014-based

Nilsen, P., Ståhl, C., Roback, K. and Cairney, P. (2013) Never the twain shall meet? –A comparison of implementation science and policy implementation research. *Implementation Science* 8: 63.

Oates, W. E. (1999) An essay on fiscal federalism. *Journal of Economic Literature*, 37(3): 1120–49.

Obinger, H., Leibfried, S. and Castles, F. (eds) (2005) *Federalism and the Welfare State. New World and European experiences.* Cambridge: Cambridge University Press.

O'Donnell, G. (2013) Fiscal policy and constitutional change. In A. Goudie (ed.) *Scotland's Future: The Economics of Constitutional Change.* Dundee: Dundee University Press, pp. 119–32.

OECD (2011) *Doing Better for Families.* Accessed at: http://www. oecd-ilibrary.org/social-issues-migration-health/doing-better-for-families_9789264098732-en

OECD (2012) *Childcare Across the OECD.* Accessed at: https://docs. google.com/spreadsheet/ccc?key=0AonYZs4MzlZbdDdCaFBjV2tX SjlGRk5mUlhDRVZJMHc

OECD (2016) *Babies and Bosses: Reconciling Work and Family Life (Vol. 4).* Accessed at: http://www.oecd-ilibrary.org/social-issues-migration-health/babies-and-bosses-reconciling-work-and-family-life-volume-4_9789264009295-en

Ohmae, K. (1995) *The End of the Nation State: The Rise of Regional Economies.* New York: The Free Press.

Orton, M. and Rowlingson, K. (2007) *Public Attitudes to Economic Inequality.* London: Joseph Rowntree Foundation.

Ostry, J. D., Berg, A. and Tsangarides, C. G. (2014) *Redistribution, Inequality, and Growth.* IMF Staff Discussion Note 14/02. Washington: International Monetary Fund.

Pascall, G. and Lewis, J. (2004) Emerging gender regimes and policies for gender equality in a wider Europe. *Journal of Social Policy*, 33(3): 373–94.

Pasquier, R. (2004) *La capacité politique des regions. Une comparaison France/Espagne.* Rennes: Presses universitaires de Rennes.

Pierson, P. (2000) Increasing returns, path dependence, and the study of politics. *The American Political Science Review*, 94(2): 251–67.

Pierson, P. (ed.) (2001) *The New Politics of the Welfare State*: Oxford: Oxford University Press.

Piketty, T. (2014) *Capital in the 21st Century*. Cambridge, MA: Harvard University Press.

Piketty, T., Saez, E. and Stantcheva, S. (2014) Optimal taxation of top labor incomes: a tale of three elasticities. *American Economic Journal: Economic Policy*, 6(1): 230–71.

Plantenga, J., Remery, C., Figueiredo, H. and Smith, M. (2009) Towards a European Union gender equality index. *Journal of European Social Policy*, 19(1): 19–33.

Pollitt, C. and Bouckaert, G. (2011) *Public Management Reform. A Comparative Analysis: New Public Management, Governance and the Neo-Weberian State*, 3rd edition. Oxford: Oxford University Press.

Porter, M. (2001) Regions and the new economics of competition. In A. J. Scott (ed.) *Global City Regions. Trends, Theory, Policy*. Oxford: Oxford University Press.

Rake, K. (ed.) (2000) *Women's Incomes over the Lifetime*. London: The Stationery Office.

Rhodes, M. (2001) The political economy of social pacts: 'competitive corporatism' and European relfare Reform. In P. Pierson (ed.) *The New Politics of the Welfare State*. Oxford: Oxford University Press.

Rhodes, M. (2013) Labour markets, welfare states and the dilemmas of European social democracy. In M. Keating and D. McCrone (eds) *The Crisis of Social Democracy in Europe*. Edinburgh: Edinburgh University Press.

Rodden, J. (2003) Reviving Leviathan: fiscal federalism and the growth of government. *International Organization*, 57(4): 695–729.

Rosie, M. and Bond, R. (2007) Social democratic Scotland? In M. Keating (ed.) *Scottish Social Democracy*. Brussels: Presses inter-universitaires européennes/Peter Lang.

Rothstein, B. (2001) The universal welfare state as a social dilemma. *Rationality and Society*, 13(2): 213–33.

Rothstein, B. and Steinmo, S. (2013) Social democracy in Crisis? What Crisis? In M. Keating and D. McCrone (eds) *The Crisis of Social Democracy in Europe*. Edinburgh: Edinburgh University Press.

Saxonberg, S. (2013) From defamilialization to degenderization: toward a new welfare typology. *Social Policy and Administration*, 47(1): 26–49.

Schmitter, P. (1974) Still the century of corporatism? *The Review of Politics*, 36(1): 85–131.

Scott, A. (1998) *Regions and the World Economy. The Coming Shape of Global Production, Competition, and Political Order*. Oxford: Oxford University Press.

Scottish Government (2011a) *The Impact of a Reduction in Corporation Tax on the Scottish Economy.* Edinburgh: Scottish Government. Accessed at: http://www.scotland.gov.uk/Resource/0038/00388940.pdf

Scottish Government (2011b) *Renewing Scotland's Public Services.* Edinburgh: Scottish Government. Accessed at: http://www.scotland.gov.uk/Publications/2011/09/21104740/0

Scottish Government (2013) *Scotland's Future: Your Guide to an Independent Scotland.* Edinburgh: Scottish Government. Accessed at: http://www.gov.scot/resource/0043/00439021.pdf

Scottish Government (2014) *The Early Years Collaborative: Stock Take Review of Years 1 and 2.* Edinburgh: Scottish Government. Accessed at: www gov.scot/Resource/0047/00473734 pdf

Scottish Government (2015a) *Creating a Fairer Scotland. Social Security: The Story So Far and the Next Steps.* Accessed at: www.gov.scot/Resource/0048/00487055.pdf

Scottish Government (2015b) *Draft Budget 2016–17.* Edinburgh: Scottish Government. Accessed at: http://www.gov.scot/Publications/2015/12/9056/20.

Scottish Government (2015c) *Programme for Government 2015–16.* Edinburgh: Scottish Government. Accessed at: http://www.gov.scot/Publications/2015/09/7685

Scottish Government (2016a) *Scottish Government Website: Wealthier and Fairer Strategic Objectives.* Edinburgh: Scottish Government. Accessed at: http://www.gov.scot/About/Performance/scotPerforms/objectives/wealthierAndFairer.

Scottish Government (2016b) *Social Security for Scotland.* Edinburgh: Scottish Government. Accessed at: http://www.gov.scot/Topics/Statistics/Browse/Social-Welfare/SocialSecurityforScotland/Social SecurityforScotland

Scottish Government (2016c) *Social Security for Scotland: Benefits Being Devolved to the Scottish Parliament.* Edinburgh: Scottish Government. Powerpoint presentation publicly available at: http://www.gov.scot/Topics/Statistics/Browse/Social-Welfare/SocialSecurityforScotland/SocialSecurityfor Scotland

Scottish Government (2016d) *Creating a Fairer Scotland. A New Future for Social Security in Scotland.* Edinburgh: Scottish Government. Accessed at: http://www.gov.scot/Topics/People/fairerscotland/future-powers/Publications/Future

Scottish Government (2016e) *Scottish Social Security. Options Appraisal Part 1: The Strategic Case for Change and the Governance of Social Security in Scotland.* Social Security Policy and Delivery and Communities Analysis, March. Edinburgh: Scottish Government. Accessed at: http://www.gov.scot/Resource/0049/00494859.pdf

Scottish Government (2016f) *Scottish Income Tax from 2017/18.*

Edinburgh: Scottish Government. Accessed at: www.gov.scot/Resource/0049/00497813.pdf

Scottish Government and ESRC (2013) *What Works Scotland (WWS)*. Accessed at: http://www.esrc.ac.uk/_images/WWS%20Call%20spec%20FINAL%2006%20Jan%202014_tcm8-29575.pdf

Scottish National Party (2016) *Manifesto 2016*. Accessed at: http://www.snp.org/manifesto

Scottish Parliament Information Centre (SPICe) (2016) *Devolution of Employment Programmes*. Briefing Paper prepared for the Devolution (Further Powers) Committee.

Smith Commission (2014) *Report of the Smith Commission for Further Devolution of Powers to the Scottish Parliament*. Accessed at: https://www.smith-commission.scot/wp-content/uploads/2014/11/The_Smith_Commission_Report-1.pdf

Soroka, S. N. and Wlezien, C. (2010) *Degrees of Democracy. Politics, Public Opinion, and Policy*. Cambridge: Cambridge University Press.

Stalker, G. and Ornstein, M. (2013) Quebec, daycare, and the household strategies of couples with young children. *Canadian Public Policy*, 39(2): 241–62.

Stiglitz, J. (2012) *The Price of Inequality*. London: Penguin.

Stiglitz, J. (2015) The origins of inequality and policies to contain it. *National Tax Journal*, 68(2): 425–48.

Sturgeon, N. (2014) Sturgeon sets out gains of independence for women. Speech to Scottish Women's Convention, Glasgow, 25 January 2014. Accessed at: http://www.snp.org/media-centre/news/2014/jan/sturgeon-sets-out-gains-independence-women

Swank, D. (2002) *Global Capital, Political Institutions and Political Change in Developed Welfare States*. Cambridge: Cambridge University Press.

Taylor-Gooby, P. (2004) *New Risks, New Welfare: The Transformation of the European Welfare State*. Oxford: Oxford University Press.

Tilly, C. (1996) *Citizenship, Identity, and Social History*. Cambridge: Cambridge University Press.

Traxler, F. (2004) The metamorphoses of corporatism: from classical to lean patterns. *European Journal of Political Research*, 43(4): 571–98.

UK Government (2013) *State of the Nation: Social Mobility and Child Poverty in Britain* (Social Mobility and Poverty Commission) Accessed at: https://www.gov.uk/government/uploads/system/uploads/attachment_data/file/292231/State_of_the_Nation_2013.pdf

UK Parliament (2016) *Scotland Act (2016)*. Accessed at: http://services.parliament.uk/bills/ 2015-16/scotland.html

Vampa, D. (2014) The sub-state politics of welfare in Italy: assessing the effect of territorial mobilization on the development of region-specific social governance. *Regional & Federal Studies*, 24(4): 473–91.

Van Lancker, W. and Ghysels, J. (2012) Great expectations, but how to achieve them? Explaining patterns of inequality in childcare use across 31 developed countries. CSB Working Paper 13/05, University of Antwerp.

Welfare Reform Committee (2016) *Welfare Reform Committee Legacy Paper: Session 4.* SP Paper 946, 3rd Report, 2016 (Session 4). Accessed at: http://www.scottish.parliament.uk/parliamentary business/CurrentCommittees/97686.aspx

White, L. A. and Friendly, M. (2012) Public funding, private delivery: states, markets, and early childhood education and care in liberal welfare states – a comparison of Australia, the UK, Quebec, and New Zealand. *Journal of Comparative Policy Analysis*, 14(4): 292–310.

Wightman, A. (2014) *A Land Value Tax for Scotland.* Accessed at: http://www.andywightman.com/docs/LVTREPORT.pdf

Wilkinson, R. and Pickett, K. (2010) *The Spirit Level: Why Equality is Better for Everyone.* Harmondsworth: Penguin.

World Bank (2014) *Prosperity for All, Ending Extreme Poverty.* World Bank Group, Paper for World Bank Group Spring Meetings (2014). Accessed at: http://siteresources.worldbank.org/INTPROSPECTS/Resources/334934-1327948020811/8401693-1397074077765/Prosperity_for_All_Final_2014.pdf

Zaller, J. R. and Feldman, S. (1992) A simple theory of the survey response: answering questions versus revealing preferences. *American Journal of Political Science*, 36(3): 579–616.

Index

Page numbers followed by 'n' are notes, 'f' are figures, and 't' are tables.